KICKASS

PRESENTATIONS

KICKASS
PRESENTATIONS

Wow Audiences with **PowerPoint Slides**
that Click, **Humor** that's Quick,
and **Messages** that Stick

DAN FRASER

SPIRIT BEAR
— BOOKS —

SPIRIT BEAR
— BOOKS —

Contact information for Spirit Bear Books: kickasspresentations@gmail.com

ISBN: 978-0-9959190-0-6 (print)
ISBN: 978-0-9959190-1-3 (ebook)

Ordering Information:
Special discounts are available on quantity purchases by corporations, associations, and others. For details, contact kickasspresentations@gmail.com

To all those who have been held hostage by a painful presentation
- may you enjoy your freedom

TABLE OF CONTENTS

YOUR WELCOME GUIDE TO KICKING ASS

Let's face it, we've all had to endure some dull, painful, and valueless presentations. Ask anyone and they'll gladly recount the agony of some train wreck of a lecture they were subjected to. I once sat through an hour-long session on financial policies where the presenter did nothing but read slides crammed full of tiny font to the audience as if we were children at bedtime. Some people got sleepy—I felt like throwing a tantrum!

There are universal things about presentations that everyone agrees are both terrible and so *not* kickass: slides filled with text (I once read that the average slide contains 40 words![1]); when the presenter reads from their slides (PowerPoint karaoke); pointless graphs; annoying animations (like when each word comes twirling in from the side)—the list goes on. Why do we do it? We all hate these things, and yet we continue to make the same mistakes over and over.

This ends with you—and it's why you need this book.

We're not deliberately trying to suck, so what's happening here? The fact is that very few people, including professional instructors, are ever trained to use software like PowerPoint *effectively*, nor are they even trained to present. How about we just copy and paste the words in the manual onto slides? Seems reasonable, right?

As an audience we all want the same thing—a clear message that is meaningful to us and is easily understood. Combine this with takeaways that are memorable and are delivered by a presenter who is professional and entertaining, and we have the makings of a *kickass presentation*.

Who Is This Book For?

Trainers, teachers, facilitators, professionals, salespeople, educators, and anyone who regularly delivers presentations—and who wants to be better at it. I deliberately use the phrase "delivering a presentation" as opposed to "giving a lecture."

A lecture conjures up, at worst, the image of a one-way conversation with an annoyed parent. At best it sounds like something you'd get from a stale professor in a tweed jacket from behind an oak podium. Either way, nobody wants to sit through it.

If you have a job, you can bet that at some point you will be asked to speak about something. This might be a short talk to a group of your peers in the boardroom or perhaps presenting a case study to hundreds of people at a business conference. Whether you're a first-time speaker or a seasoned professional, this book will offer checklists and tips for presenters at every level.

How to Use This Book

This book is intended to be used as a tool. Read it from cover to cover if you wish (nerd!), but most people won't, and you don't need to. Skim the headlines and stop at what you find interesting or where you think the smallest change will make the biggest impact. Highlight, write in the margin, and mark it up with sticky notes. Ideally, you should *have it with you while you build your presentation.* If you can use a concept you like to make your presentations better, that's a win. Hopefully, this will find its way to your work desk or somewhere near your laptop, but if it ends up in the bathroom, that's fine too. I've intentionally made the pages glossy enough that they make for terrible wipes.

Chapter 1

IT'S NOT ABOUT YOU!

***You* Are the Presentation—But It's Not about You**

The audience does not need to tune themselves to you—you need to tune your message to them. Skilled presenting requires you to understand their hearts and minds and create a message to resonate with what's already there.

—Nancy Duarte[2]

Let me be clear—*you* are the presentation! People are there to see you and to hear what you have to say. Your slides and visual aids simply enhance your message. This means that you must master your content and have your message dialed in. It also means that the audience should be primarily focused on you—your facial expressions, body language, hand gestures, eye contact, the words you say, and how you say them. Gone are the days of standing behind a lectern and gripping the sides as if it's going to float away. People want to see you and your unique way of delivering your message. This doesn't mean bouncing around or getting overly excited—it means being your authentic self, who is present in the moment.

I once had the privilege of seeing author Malcolm Gladwell speak to a packed theater audience. Gladwell is very reserved. He doesn't shout, jump around, or even have an animated face. Despite this, his passion for his topic was so evident that he had thousands of people hanging on his every word. He had no pictures, video, music, or sparklers—*he* was the presentation.

I've attended a few classes where the presenter simply sat in a chair at the front or, worse, at the back of the room! How do you expect your audience to be engaged if you're not? It's pretty tough to be a kickass presenter from this position. Later in the book, we'll look at some of these behaviors and discuss how to ramp up your effectiveness.

Even though you are the presentation, realize that it's not about you, *it's about your audience*—their issues, their concerns, their questions, and their needs.

Don't Show Them What You Can Do—Show Them What They Can Do

Early in my police career, I attended a knife-fighting seminar (for real!). The instructor showed off some complex ninja-like moves that left the class befuddled and frustrated. He was highly skilled, but he wasn't able, or willing, to put his own ego aside and teach anything meaningful to new people.

This isn't *America's Got Talent*. What you can do as an expert might be very impressive, but your audience isn't you. It's great to provide a perfect demonstration of where your students might get to if they practice. What's now easy for you may not be for them. Throughout my teaching I've caught myself falling into this same trap. If you see that your students are overwhelmed or not picking up what you're teaching them, the problem likely lies with you.

The key is to break down your message into chunks that your audience can digest at whatever level they're at. Provide them with steps and the road map that they will need to be successful.

Find Out What Matters to Them and Get to It Quickly

If you're speaking to people in your industry, this can be pretty easy. However, I've been asked to speak to audiences that are just on the fringe of being able to apply what I normally teach. By asking questions about their needs, issues, and level of knowledge well beforehand, you're better able to tailor your message directly to them as opposed to subjecting them to a presentation that was built for an entirely different audience.

We've all sat through presentations given by someone who we didn't know existed before they started talking. They quickly establish themselves as the only ones who know anything—leaving you, the audience, as the ones who know nothing. They have the attention of the group, and they want everyone to know it. Don't be that presenter. Remember that it's not your audience's job to care about you; it's your job to care about them. Make it about them—make them the heroes. Empower them to leave the room and be more effective in their own lives, whether professional or personal.

The Attention Span of a Goldfish—Really?

Much has been said about the evils of technology and how it has contributed to the downfall of our society's ability to concentrate. A study conducted by Microsoft on 2,000 Canadians reported that, in 2013, people lost their concentration after eight seconds. This was a drastic decline from their study in 2000 that showed an attention span of 12 seconds.[3]

It is often said that a goldfish has an attention span of only nine seconds.[4] *I checked and they're talking about the actual fish and not the yummy cracker. Whew!* Bring on the fantastical click-bait headlines about how the freakin' fish have us beat by a whole second. Let's pump the brakes on this for a second so that presenters everywhere don't feel doomed.

I have no idea how anyone would measure goldfish attention spans. I'm no marine biologist, but I think what they really mean is that a goldfish has a memory that lasts only nine seconds. Fair enough. What the study on humans really means is that people will click away from a website or video after only eight seconds if the content isn't engaging. Thankfully, a presentation is not a web page or a piece of social media, so there's no need to hustle through our material as if we're trying to stay on a rodeo bull.

The next thing we have to contend with is the arbitrary 10- to 15-minute attention span rule[5] (think time between TV commercial breaks). The actual research data on this is hard to quantify. When I was in the military, all presentations were broken into 40-minute sessions based on the theory that no one can sit for any longer than that in one stretch and still be attentive. Seems plausible, but how do you account for movies? A great film will hold us spellbound for two plus hours. We've all been in presentations that make us want to stick a #2 pencil in our eye after five minutes and others that have us wanting more, even after six hours.

> "The brain doesn't pay attention to boring things."
> —John Medina, *Brain Rules*[6]

Over the last decade, adults have come to expect some entertainment along with their information, so don't be boring! Ok, we get it! But how? We need to be better at injecting emotion—humor, fear, surprise, fun, anger, wonder … you get the picture. As speakers and educators, we need to rise to the challenge and deliver what we'd want to experience ourselves as members of an audience. Harness the techniques in this book and take your presentations to a level that kicks ass!

Chapter Takeaways

1. *You* are the presentation—not your slides.
2. Your presentation is not about you; it's about your audience's needs.

3. Show the audience what *they* can do with the information you present.

4. It's not the audience's job to care about you—it's your job to care about them.

5. We keep our audience engaged with emotion—techniques for this will be covered later in the book.

Chapter 2

FAIL TO PLAN, PLAN TO FAIL

Have you ever been in a presentation where you thought to yourself, "Wow, this presenter really knows their stuff?" If so, you also know that you're likely to be more forgiving of them if they don't demonstrate great delivery behaviors, such as eye contact, voice projection, and body language. This is because they are experts on their material, not professional presenters.

The opposite is not true. Someone might have all the speaking skills down, but if they don't know what they're talking about, the audience tunes them out quickly. We have to have *substance* before we can add *sparkle*.

The best way to prevent a presentation train wreck is to do the hard work long before the moment you walk on stage. As a young soldier, I learned the seven *P*s: Proper preparation and planning prevents piss-poor performance. This means that you'd better know your stuff.

Master Your Content

You need to know your content in far greater depth than the level at which you're presenting and know it better than almost anyone in the audience. This is *foundational* to being a kickass presenter. Only once you have mastered your content can you tailor it to the individuals in your audience.

Leadership trainer and *Manager Tools* podcaster Mark Horstman uses this great analogy: Many presenters feel that they have reached "black belt" status in presenting when they've mastered their content. The reality is that, in martial arts, reaching black-belt level means that you're just starting to learn.[7]

> **"Everyone wants to be an instructor until it's time to do instructor shit."**
>
> —Will Petty, Centrifuge Training[8]

The journey to mastering your content will take time and effort. It will likely mean not just having real-world experience in your topic but also reading books, articles, research summaries, and blog posts as part of your ongoing research. It means watching videos, attending seminars and conferences, speaking with experts, and listening to podcasts. It means putting in the hours of rehearsal and *purposeful practice* at the task of presenting that so many people hate—and therefore don't do. It doesn't need to become an obsession, but it should be more than just a hobby.

It will mean you consider all angles of your topic including ones that may fly in the face of your current opinion and even make your blood boil.

In the late 2000s, I was working toward becoming the lead Taser instructor for my police department. At the time, the weapon was relatively new, and there was debate and controversy in the media almost daily. The police would speak of research and lessons learned through real-world use, and this stance would be held up as equal to nearly anyone they could find with a passionate opinion to the contrary. Reading some of these articles made me hiss like an angry kettle, but I forced myself to consider the opinions of those on the other side of the issue from me. This kept me not only well informed but also guarded against confirmation bias—the tendency to take in, interpret, and recall information in a way that confirms your established beliefs.

True mastery comes when you know your material so well that you no longer need to give it conscious thought. This frees up space in your mind to focus on your actual presentation skills and, therefore, to fully pay attention to the experience your audience is having and to adapt how you deliver your message *based on their reaction.*

Are there people in your audience who seem disengaged (staring at their phones), agitated, or even angry? How are you going to know this if you're busy reading off the slides, reading from your notes, or staring at the floor while stressing over what to say next? This is the real reason for making eye contact—to connect with individuals in the audience and notice what they are experiencing. This then gives you the opportunity to address what you see.

Here's a litmus test: If you have to look at your slides to know what to say next, then you haven't mastered your content. The minimum is knowing what you're going to say, knowing what's on your slides, and being confident in answering any questions that arise from either. That is *what* you are presenting. You must also deeply understand the *why*—the principles that underlie your material. Why are you speaking about this subject? Why is it important to your audience?

For example, let's say you decide to show a video of a real-life incident. Do you know the background and context, and can you speak to it without notes? When and where did it occur? Who are the people involved? What was the outcome? What factors affect your perception of the situation? How does the video relate to this particular audience? Dig into the background, read everything you can about it, and talk to the people involved if possible. Anticipate the questions you're likely to get from the audience, and work to answer them as part of your presentation before they are asked.

How Do I Get Better at Presenting?

> **When the master is no longer the student, he is no longer the master.**
>
> —Proverb

The fact that you're even reading this book is a good step. Reading books, watching tutorials, taking seminars, and attending conferences will make you a better presenter. However, you can read all the books you want, but ultimately, *there is no substitute for stage time.* Presenting is a physical skill. Just like golf, you're not going to get to the Masters by watching it on TV—you have to get out there and hit the ball.

Seize opportunities to get in front of an audience. Does your workplace need first-aid instructors? Is the local Rotary Club looking for someone to speak at a meeting? Jump on these opportunities. I see no one hungrier to get in front of an audience than new-on-the-scene comedians. They will go to comedy clubs several nights a week, just hoping to be picked to go on for five minutes! I've seen comedians drive three hours for a paltry seven minutes of stage time (I know this because I was one of them). They understand that this is how you get better.

For years I had several recurring short talks that I would deliver to athletes at a local running store. At times there were 20 people in the audience, but often there were fewer. One evening I set up the seating and my white-board, only to find a lone woman in the audience. I had a choice: I could have easily canceled, but instead, I looked at it as an opportunity to find out what was important to her and to get right down to providing something that was valuable to her.

In Malcolm Gladwell's excellent book *Outliers: The Story of Success,* he presents research that shows that it takes 10 thousand hours of concentrated practice to become a master in anything. Quoting psychologist Daniel Levitin:

> The emerging picture from such studies is that ten thousand hours of practice is required to achieve the level of mastery associated with being a world-class expert—in anything... In study after study, of composers, basketball players, fiction writers, ice skaters, concert pianists, chess players, master criminals, and what have you, this number comes up again

and again. Of course, this doesn't address why some people get more out of their practice sessions than others do. But no one has yet found a case in which true world-class expertise was accomplished in less time. It seems that it takes the brain this long to assimilate all that it needs to know to achieve true mastery.[9]

I know what you're thinking: "But, I have a presentation to deliver next month, and I don't have ten thousand hours!" You're right—and that's ok. No one expects you to be kickass right out of the gate. The reality is that you'd have to practice an activity 40 hours a week for five years to get the hours you need. That doesn't mean just doing the activity but practicing it—doing it purposefully with the goal of being better tomorrow than you are today.

Who could possibly get in 10 thousand hours of speaking time in five years? Teachers, for one. How many teachers have world-class presentation skills after five, 10, or even 20 years? The answer is very few. The reason is that like most people, they're just doing their job. They're not all practicing with the goal of improving. Will they get better? Of course. Would they get better faster if they were constantly evaluating their performance and being coached along the way? You bet.

Are you taking every opportunity you can to speak in front of people? When you do, are you taking the time to look back over your performance to see where you can be better next time? Are you seeking feedback? More on this in chapter 9.

Print Your Slides and Practice with Them

Technology is a bit of a double-edged sword. Used right, it's a wonderful tool, but unfortunately, it makes it easier for a lot of mediocre people to get really crappy ideas out.

—Martin Gore[10]

*This is me one early morning on a flight to speak in
Wyoming. Not much room for a laptop anyway!*

Being the master of your content will make you a more confident, kickass speaker and won't derail you when your technology fails—and eventually it will. Part of being a skilled presenter means having a hard copy of your slides printed off and being prepared to use them. If you are using mostly pictures, you can print many slides on a page and use it as a quick-glance handrail to keep you on track. The trick is making sure that you practice with this method. That means literally running through your talk with your printed slide papers within view. Without your slides, how can you use body language, props, or even a whiteboard to get your point across? Speaking coach Fred E. Miller calls having a back-up plan your "spare tire." Having a spare tire and knowing how to use it are two different things.[11]

Ultimately, you cannot be the judge of whether or not you've mastered your content—the audience and its perception of you are the final judges.

You may be tested in the form of questions or challenges on your material and its underlying principles. The audience's feedback will be your best indication of your level of mastery.

I once attended a presentation at a national-level conference where the presenter had flown in from another country to speak. She started off by telling everyone that this was not her material and that she was using a presentation she'd been given by a colleague. She then reacted to each slide as something she had never seen before and simply spoke a bit about each one.

People in the audience shifted uncomfortably in their seats as she muddled her way through it. At one point she mentioned a magazine article that she read on the plane on the way to the conference. All I could think was, "She should have been learning this presentation on the plane instead of reading some random magazine." Her credibility—and that of her organization—was lost, as was the opportunity to make a meaningful impact.

What Does Your Audience Want?

Let's start with the most important thing—*what matters to them*. If you don't know what this is, you may just be wasting everyone's time. Often this has been answered for you by the fact that you've been asked to present a particular topic to the group. Someone who knows the audience and their needs feels that what you've got to teach them is valuable. For most presentations a formal needs assessment isn't necessary.

From here you can continue to dial in on individual audience members if circumstances and time permit. Here are a few methods:

1. Talk to audience members well before the presentation starts. This might be days or weeks beforehand, in person or by email: "Hey, Michelle, I'll be speaking to your team next week about communication skills. What are you most hoping to get out of it? What challenges have you faced in this area?"

2. Get there early and have a few short conversations with audience members in the minutes before you begin. Ask some questions like, "What's your experience with this?" or "What are you hoping to learn?" This is a great way to banter with your audience and lead into certain topics. "Joe and I were chatting earlier, and he mentioned that knowing more about how people communicate in emails would be a valuable skill to have. Let's look at that now."

3. Ask the audience some questions near the beginning of the presentation, either through a group-brainstorming session where you write people's answers on a flip chart or have them fill out index cards and hand them in. Ask some simple questions like, "What are you hoping to learn more about?" Go over these questions with the audience right away and then come back to them at the end.

4. Ask questions of individual audience members at the beginning of the session. If you're in a smaller group where people are introducing themselves, you can ask them then what they want to get out of the training, what questions they hope to have answered, etc. Write them down and revisit them at the end.

If you can't address their question or issue in the presentation itself, you can refer them to some resources. All these methods help personalize the content and generate buy-in.

Where Do I Even Start?

I begin many of my presentations with this question to the audience: "What is the goal of training?" This is a tougher question than it appears. Most people answer with things like "to learn something new," "to expand the mind," or "to get better." Though these are good answers, they're not what I'm looking for. What if you attend a presentation where the speaker wows you with all kinds of mind-blowing new information, but then you leave and continue doing exactly what you did before? What was the point? (By the way, the same goes for reading a book like this.)

As I see it, the goal of training is to *change people's behavior*. If you attend a training session where you hear and see nothing new, but you then go out into the world and put these ideas into practice, that is more valuable than new knowledge that you never use. We can easily become "parent deaf" by hearing the same message from the same person. Sometimes all it takes to spark new behavior is hearing a similar message from someone new.

When designing a presentation, many trainers simply take the content they have (often from documents like policy manuals) and start dumping it into a PowerPoint without a clear sense of their goal—what they want their audience to walk away knowing or doing differently.

I'd love to sit here and tell you that I've been clear and systematic in de- signing every presentation and training program I've ever delivered, but that's not even close to the truth. I've often inherited presentations from someone else. When this happens, it can be tough to innovate and find a new and better way of delivering it.

When designing an original program, the material has to come from somewhere, and it never seems to come all at once or in any structured sequence. You'll likely have ideas for various parts of the presentation: text, images, video, activities, quotes, and even stories. But what do you do with it all? Don't worry—this starting point is pretty common, and that's ok. Dr. Sivasailam "Thiagi" Thiagarajan does a nice job of providing a frame- work for thinking about this. His analogy is to imagine four shoeboxes labeled *objectives, activities, content,* and *test items*.[12]

As ideas come to you about parts of a presentation, imagine that you fill out a recipe card and toss it into the appropriate box. In reality you'll be better off making a note in a file on your phone or computer. As any comedian will tell you, when you get an idea, you've got to write it down right away, or like trying to hang on to a slippery fish, it'll be gone. Once a solid idea is in a "box," you'll then need to address it in the other three boxes.

So let's say you're putting together a presentation on preserving elephant habitats in Botswana. You come across some great information about how much land is required to sustain one elephant. You feel that this is an important bit of *content*, so now you need to create an *objective* for it. For example, "At the end of this presentation you'll be able to define the land mass, in square miles, required to sustain one adult elephant." You may want to develop an *activity* that incorporates this or include it in an activity, such as in an end-of-presentation review. Finally, you may want to ask a *test question*.

> **"If you don't know what you want to achieve in your presentation your audience never will."**
>
> —Harvey Diamond[13]

Begin with the End in Mind

Where are we going with this presentation? If the top of the mountain is the goal, where are we now, and what steps do we need to take to get there?

As a police trainer, I once got a call from an officer in the US who had been tasked with delivering de-escalation training to officers in his state. He asked my advice on what type of content to include. There were two problems with his request: (a) He had no clear objectives, and (b) he wanted to do it all through online learning. I explained to him that even with clearly defined objectives he would have a hard time achieving them through e-learning because talking to people is a physical skill—it can't be effectively taught through videos or reading.

Much like with archery, decorating a cake, or operating a backhoe, you have to physically do it—preferably with proper coaching—to get good at it. I explained to the officer that my department had a 40-hour training program, which starts off with a classroom presentation but also involves lots of practice and a heavy dose of role-playing scenarios. He was not happy with that answer. I'm sure he hoped that I would be able to simply email him some slides and videos and his work would be mostly done.

It is not uncommon to inherit a presentation or even a whole training program from someone else. If the objectives weren't clear for the past trainer, then this is where you need to start.

Define Your Objective

If your audience could leave knowing only one thing, what would it be? If your audience only remembered one thing from your presentation in a year or five years from now, what would it be? If they could leave and just do one thing differently, what would it be? Taking the time to clarify these questions will help you to focus on the most important concepts when designing your presentation. This is called backward integrated design—a fancy way of saying, "Let's figure out where we want to end up and then work out how we'll get there."

So … what's your objective? Imagine a team of bad-ass special operations soldiers climbing into a helicopter for a mission, bristling with weapons, armor, and Velcro. Do you think they have a clear objective? Of course! Your presentation is no different (except for maybe less Velcro).

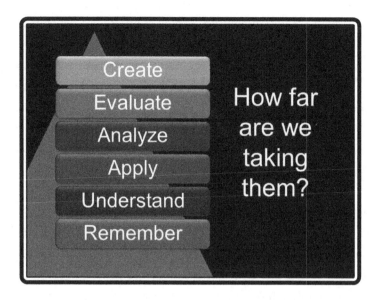

This little pyramid is called Bloom's Taxonomy[14]—and if you're like me, your eyes just glazed over a bit. Bloom's may not be sexy, but it is important. It's been around since the 1950s and helps educators to create achievable learning goals. It starts low on the mountain with students simply being able to remember certain important things and moves up to them being able to do things like combine elements of a problem to form new solutions.

In most presentations we're looking at objectives in the *first three steps*. This is where it becomes important to know your audience, where they're at, and what they need and expect from you.

Here are some words that will be useful when coming up with your objectives:

> *Remember*—define, label, list, name, recall, select, find
> *Understand*—explain, classify, illustrate, outline, summarize, discuss
> *Apply*—utilize, build, develop, select, construct, calculate, draw
> *Analyze*—examine, distinguish, compare, test for, discover, organize
> *Evaluate*—assess, defend, influence, prioritize, support, critique
> *Create*—design, develop, improve, plan, modify

Don't discount the importance of simple memorization. I remember struggling through learning my times tables as a kid. Teachers used to say, "You need to know this because you're not always going to be walking around with a calculator in your pocket." *A-hem*. Knowing your times tables is still an important foundational skill, whether you have access to a calculator or not. Why? Because it frees up *mental space* to do more complex things. If you have to pull out your phone every time you need to know what 9 × 9 is, the process of working through your larger problem just got much slower.

Are new police officers immediately forced to memorize the radio 10-code system of their department? That's a big 10–4! Couldn't they just refer to a laminated card in their pocket with all the codes on them? Sure, but it would slow their ability to communicate, to be agile, and to think their way creatively through more complex and time-sensitive problems. Being able to effortlessly recall the basics is at the base of Bloom's pyramid for a reason.

Learning objectives are an important part of planning a presentation. Standard learning objectives are brief statements that describe what students will be expected to learn by the end of the presentation or training session. They provide both you and your students with a road map of where you intend to go. They also allow you to measure your success (at least in the short term) through testing.

Here are some examples:

"At the end of this session, students will be able to recognize and describe the signs of someone having a stroke."

"At the end of this session, students will be able to explain the phases of the moon and their effects on the world's oceans."

"At the end of this session, students will be able to tie a bowline knot."

A kickass presentation has *clearly defined objectives.*

Clearly Identify Your Learning Objectives and Write Them Down

Though this may seem like a boring activity, it will save you time in the end. Your clearly defined learning objectives will act like a compass needle for your preparation and, later, for your audience. You should *regularly refer back to your objectives* to make sure that you haven't wandered offtrack and into the rhubarb.

Who cares? Once you have clear objectives, you need to communicate to the audience why they should care. Tune them into WIIFM—what's in it for me? How is what you're teaching them going to benefit them or make their lives easier? How can they use it to avoid pain? When exactly are they going to use the information? We'll talk more about this in chapter 6.

Remember, the audience is there to see you, not your slides! The information, stories, experience, and knowledge are in your head—now we just need to figure out how to get it into theirs. You may not need any technology at all. Not every presentation needs an accompanying PowerPoint. In fact, two of the most effective speakers I know, Gordon Graham and Lt. Col. (Ret.) Dave Grossman, don't even use PowerPoint. Both deliver engaging daylong training sessions using nothing but an old-school overhead projector and a flip chart. So, when you have identified your learning objectives, think about what media will get your point across most effectively.

It's difficult to get away from presentation software like PowerPoint or Keynote. If you decide to use one of these programs, the first thing to do is step away from the computer. Wait, what? That's right—step away from the computer.

Even with defined objectives, it's still tempting to just start dumping content into slides. Instead, use paper, or even sticky notes or recipe cards, to map out your presentation. Get your takeaway messages down on paper first and only then decide on what images, video, audio clips, stories, props, diagrams, and activities will best communicate them.

Why PowerPoint?

The bulk of this book will refer to Microsoft PowerPoint because it's the most widely used presentation software in the world. I started using PowerPoint in the mid-1990s while working in the Canadian Armed Forces. Though the program had been around for a few years at that time, it was still the early days of presentation software and digital images were hard to come by. One of my jobs as an instructor in the army was to begin transferring the content from transparencies for overhead projectors into this new visual medium.

Throughout my career in government, PowerPoint has been the default. People who are passionate about their computers are happy to debate the merits of one program over another. Regardless, the concepts that I'll address here are fairly universal and can be applied whether you're using Apple Keynote, Google Slides, Prezi, or whatever software pops up in the near future as an alternative.

What audiences loathe above all else are terrible presentations. I've never had someone come up to me after a presentation and say, "That was great, I just hate that you used PowerPoint." PowerPoint is simply a tool, like a hammer. However, it's not always the right tool for the job. Some people see every presentation as a nail and would never consider not using it. Some audience members have learned to fear it because they've been smashed in the face with it for years. Your job is to wield PowerPoint so effectively that your audience doesn't even have the chance to start hating.

If people so despise PowerPoint, why do we continue to use it? Here's why:

- Its powerful editing capabilities let you create visual displays of information and concepts.
- It allows simple integration of video and audio.
- It documents what you've taught.

- It allows you to keep detailed speaker notes and create handouts.
- It's portable.
- It lets you share information.

Within PowerPoint, single pages are called *slides* and all the slides together form a *deck* (think deck of cards). This goes back to when 35mm pictures were displayed on transparent slides that were loaded into a round carousel and projected onto a screen. I still remember sitting on the plastic-covered sofa in my great-aunt's living room as a child and enduring her seemingly endless slides from a vacation to Hawaii. To this day, the word "slide" still makes me think of roasted pig and blue-haired seniors in grass skirts.

So, you've decided to use PowerPoint—now to kick ass with it!

You know what you want to achieve, and you know your key takeaway messages. Now your job is to build a deck that is visually pleasing while effectively communicating your message. Chapter 3 will walk you through this.

Understanding Copyright

I'm not a lawyer, and this is not legal advice. Please check the laws for where you live before you use an image or video that is not your own. Just because you're using it for educational purposes or have cited your sources, it doesn't give you carte blanche. Copyright law can be very complicated, and like all laws, they are moving targets that change often. Whenever you can, use images that you own, have a Creative Commons license, or are royalty free.

Should I Show a Video?

You're building a presentation and come across a video that you think might be good to include. Video can be a great way to add value and variety to your presentation, but first you need to know exactly why you're using it. The key to video is that it must be completely *relevant to your topic and audience*. When considering one for use, watch it at least five times and look for all the ways it relates to your message. Before you decide to include a video, here are some questions to ask yourself:

1. Does it reinforce a key message? A video should add to your message—but it shouldn't *be* the message.
2. Does it add context or help to explain a concept?
3. Does it add humor or evoke another useful emotional response? (In the past I've used an uplifting video at the end of a presentation on a tough subject.)
4. Is it too long? Keep everyone engaged by using videos that are under one minute. The longer a video is, the less chance that what's in it is still completely relevant to your topic. Learn to edit video so that you can cut out everything except what you want to show.
5. Does it show the audience the right way to handle a situation? This is an important concept in training for skills that people must perform under stress. If you're training pilots on emergency procedures, for example, you're setting them up for failure by showing a video of other pilots screwing up or making less-desirable decisions.

How to Kick Ass with Video

Gen Xers like me will remember the hit of pure joy and excitement when the teacher would wheel in a cart with a TV and a VHS player. Video time! Students love video, and its power hasn't changed. It's easier now than ever to find relevant video content and present it in a compelling way.

So, you've got a great video clip that will add to your presentation. Here are my tips for kickass video use:

1. Save the video file on your computer. Whenever possible, don't rely on a link to YouTube or some other site. Not only is it disruptive to the flow of your presentation, but I've been that presenter who clicked on their video hyperlink only to discover that

the video was no longer available. Fail! There are several software programs out there that let you download video from sites like YouTube.

2. Keep the video in the same file folder as the PowerPoint. Videos are not always truly embedded in the software, so PowerPoint must know where to look for the video. Keep the file path to the video as short as possible, and remember that videos may need to be relinked when using a flash drive.

3. Make the video a seamless part of your presentation. Go to the Playback tab, set the video to "Start: Automatically" and also "Play full screen." A nice way to set this up is to have a slide prior to the video that allows you to introduce it. Then you can advance the slide with your remote and have it play full screen when you're ready.

4. Test your video in the room you'll be using to ensure everything, including the audio, runs smoothly. Test the lighting to ensure that your visuals are clear and sharp.

5. Before you press Play, introduce the video, pointing out to the audience why it's relevant and what they should pay particular attention to. This is where knowing some background details of the video will pay off, especially if it's a video of a real-life event.

6. Once the video starts playing, have a look to see if you need to move the cursor off the screen. It's distracting for everyone if the little icon happens to be sitting on someone's nostril.

7. Know how and where to pause the video if there are appropriate discussion points along the way. This works great for videos of real-life events or where there are important points worth addressing.

8. Be ready with what you're going to say when the video ends. For example, what questions will you ask the audience? Videos rarely speak for themselves, so be ready to use what the audience just saw to reinforce your own message.

Get a Presentation Remote!

A presentation remote is a small gadget you carry in your hand that connects wirelessly to your computer and allows you to advance slides from anywhere in the room.

It boggles my mind how many presenters opt not to use one. A kickass presenter can't be handcuffed to the computer. I've seen presenters carry a wireless mouse with them and try awkwardly to click the correct button as they speak. I've seen presenters stand (or worse, sit!) next to their laptop and advance the slides manually from the keyboard. Perhaps the most annoying is when they have another person advance the slides for them. They look in their helper's direction each time and say, "Ok, next slide." Not professional and certainly not kickass.

Buy yourself a simple remote—this is a small investment with a huge payoff. The most basic remote will go forward and backward in your deck and will also have a laser pointer. They're relatively cheap—I carry two of them. I was once presenting when I fumbled my remote and saw it break into multiple pieces on the tile floor. I pulled out my spare and was back up and running in under 20 seconds. Two is one and one is none.

No Brown M&Ms

> **"If you don't have a process, you're making it up as you go, performance is mixed, outcomes are harder to predict, causes of success and failure are harder to isolate."**
>
> —Mark Horstman, Manager Tools[15]

Checklists, as simple and as boring as they may seem, save us from making avoidable errors and help to improve performance. Pilots, surgeons, soldiers, and executives use them—and so should we.

Many people associate a musician's request of "no brown M&Ms in the dressing room" with being a high-maintenance diva. What many don't realize is that this is actually a clever safety procedure.

In the 1980s, superstar rock band Van Halen traveled with the biggest stage production in history. They were setting up in arenas that had never had to accommodate such a heavy stage, or a ceiling that had never been adorned with 850 giant PAR lamps. Along with this huge production came a very thick checklist of technical and safety procedures that the venue had to get right for the show. In the middle of this long checklist, explained band member David Lee Roth, was this: "There will be no brown M&Ms in the backstage area, or the promoter will forfeit the show at full pay."[16]

When the band arrived, they could look at the bowl of M&Ms on the catering table and know immediately if the fine details of the checklist had been followed. If the bowl still contained brown M&Ms, it meant two things: first they would trash the dressing room to get the promoter's attention, and then they would do a thorough walk-through to see what else the venue had failed to do.

Checklists ensure that we're getting the basic things right. If we can't do that, then who knows what else we're missing?

Presentation Checklist

You've looked over your slides and are happy with them. Now it's time to take a broader view of your presentation and slide deck.

1. You've memorized your purposeful opener.
2. Your identified objectives are met.
3. Your takeaway messages are clear.
4. You've used the FASST acronym (at least in part) to ensure that your ideas are sticky. Don't worry, we'll cover this in chapter 4.
   a. Feelings
   b. Analogies

      c. Surprise

      d. Stories

      e. Tangible

5. You've injected humor.

6. You've built in a review to summarize your objectives (if appropriate).

7. Video and audio run smoothly.

8. You've memorized your purposeful close.

*You'll find all the checklists again at the end of the book.

Gear Check!

You wouldn't scuba dive, go camping, or even take your kids to their dance recital without a list of all the gear you'll need, and presenting is no different.

Get there early! I cannot stress this enough. Getting to an unfamiliar venue an hour before you speak will give you time to set everything up and run some tests (like sound) before the audience is in their seats. Being early will also let you settle in and will free you up to meet and greet people as they come in.

> ### "Men have become the tools of their tools."
> —Henry David Thoreau[17]

The more technology involved in your presentation, the more opportunities there are for one of those things to fail. I've seen it happen. I was at an event where the speaker had forwarded his presentation by email to an event volunteer ahead of time and assumed that it would all be ready for him when he arrived. The event volunteer assumed that the speaker would bring his own computer or flash drive. The result was an awkwardly late start, followed by a muddled 90-minute talk using only a flip chart. The entire time the speaker kept saying, "I wish I had my slideshow here ..." Presentation fail!

"Always plan for the fact that no plan
ever goes according to plan."

—Simon Sinek[18]

Here's a quick *equipment checklist*, especially useful for when you're presenting off-site:

1. Your entire presentation on a *flash drive* in case your laptop crashes.

2. Your *laptop* in case the venue's computer crashes.

3. A *presentation remote* (and a back-up with extra batteries!)

4. Any *adapter cables* you might need, for example: HDMI to VGA.

5. An *extension cord* and *power bar.*

6. A *small high-quality speaker*—don't rely entirely on the venue's sound system.

7. If you need internet access, make sure you have a back-up plan, like turning your phone into a *Wi-Fi hotspot.*

8. Your entire presentation *printed out* so that if all else fails, you can still go ahead without technology.

9. *Props*, handouts, games, extra dry-erase markers, and any other odds and sods.

*You'll find all the checklists again at the end of the book.

What Do I Wear?

There's a great rule that I learned from body language expert Jim Zalud at a seminar in 2012: Dress 10 percent better than your audience. This rule has never served me wrong. Think about it. If you're speaking to a group of people wearing t-shirts and jeans, you might look well out of place in a three-piece suit. You want to be relatable to your audience, so the goal is to look like you're one of them (though just a touch more dapper)—not above them. I've given many presentations where wearing a suit would have been just weird. Of course, there's always an exception—if you're a homicide detective speaking to a university class, a suit is what they expect.

You need to *feel comfortable* and *confident* in whatever you're wearing to speak in. If you have a dress that looks amazing on you but has a tag that scratches at your neck, leave it in the closet (or cut that tag off!). Those shoes that are so stylish but squeeze your pinky toe—not today. Having a few great outfits at varying levels of dressiness is just one less thing to worry about and allows you to focus on being your best. Ditch the jingly jewelry and the keys in your pocket. While you're at it, silence your phone and leave it out of sight.

The Rehearsal

"Be Prepared."

Scout Motto
—Robert Baden-Powell[19]

Imagine that tomorrow you've got an interview for your dream job, or a music concert in front of a live audience, or a wedding! It's a no-brainer that we go over what we're going to do, in as realistic a setting as possible. If it's important—and especially if we don't do it often—we must rehearse.

If there's one area where presenters fall down, it's right here. We've all been on the receiving end of a presenter who we wished had just gone over their stuff. If you want to kick ass, here's how to get it right:

1. Do it *out loud*. If you think that you can just say it in your head—or worse, just look through your slides—you are not preparing effectively. Presenting is a physical skill, so stand up and get your whole body involved. If you're going to be using a handheld mic, then grab a pen, a toothbrush, or an empty toilet paper roll to practice with.

2. Whenever possible, practice in the room you'll be speaking in. This allows you to test and set up your equipment, see how much space you have to move around in, imagine the audience in their seats, and see what your slides look like from the back of the room.

3. If you can't use the room you'll be in, do your best with what you have. I've spent countless hours talking to the walls of my hotel room, presentation remote in hand, and imagining that my laptop screen is a projection screen.

4. For speeches and formal presentations, you may want to time yourself. If you flub something, just keep going and fix it on the fly as you will in your actual talk.

5. Use video. It's hard to read the label when you're inside the bottle. You can learn a lot from seeing yourself speak on video that you won't get from simply delivering your talk in front of a mirror. I know, no one wants to watch themselves speak on video, but it's a great way to get better fast. On video there's no hiding the "ums" and "ahs" or denying that you spoke to what looks like two ladies in the front row while ignoring the rest of the audience. The video doesn't lie, and you're not likely to get more honest feedback.

The Word Whisker

You know those little filler noises like "um," "ah," and the prolific "like"? Those are bad, but some make me want to start flipping tables. Ever been stuck listening to someone who can't get through a sentence without an "obviously," "apparently," or "basically"? We say them without conscious awareness. I've been caught doing this myself, and I've worked hard to banish them. Oh no! Do you have one? What should you do about it?

Step 1 Awareness: use video or rehearse in front of someone who will point it out. A fun (for them) game is to have someone ring a bell, honk a horn, or clang a pot whenever you use a word whisker in rehearsal. You can do this while running through your presentation material or just speaking on a random topic for 60 seconds.

Step 2 Just stop it! Slow your rate of speech. When you get the urge to say "um" or "ah," just be silent instead. You can, like, trust me on that. ;-)

Chapter Takeaways

1. Master your content and practice with no technology.
2. Get out there and do it. There is no substitute for stage time.
3. Dress in something that makes you feel comfortable and confident.
4. Use an equipment checklist and get to the venue early.
5. Find out what's important to the audience and get to it quickly.
6. Clearly define your presentation objectives.
7. If you're going to use PowerPoint, have a good reason for doing so.
8. If you plan to show a video, make the integration seamless.
9. Use a presentation remote.
10. Rehearse out loud.

Exercise

Pull out a presentation that you plan to give, define the objectives, and write them down. This may take a few minutes to complete but will be worth the effort. These objectives can now be used to ensure that you've got content, activities, and test items that are all in alignment.

Chapter 3

DESIGNING A KICKASS SLIDE

So, you sit down to start building your slide deck. You open PowerPoint, and bang! What do you get? A blank screen with a title box and a spot for bullet points underneath. All you need to do now is add your title and as many bullet points as you can dream up! Or why not just cut and paste blocks of text from a manual!

Don't fall for it—it's a trap! Do you want Death by PowerPoint? Because that is how you get Death by PowerPoint.

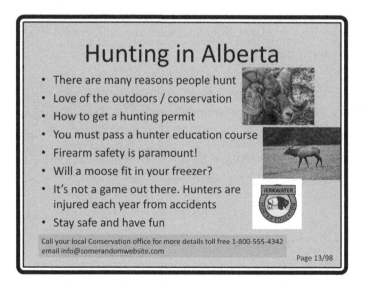

This is how to build terrible slides: Start with the title; slap in some text for the bullet points; there's room at the bottom so let's add some more info, the page number ... There's still some room! Let's cram in some pictures!

Get the Show on the Road

Imagine you're driving in an unfamiliar city. You're cruising down a freeway searching for your exit when you look up to see ... this? The sign might contain some great information, but there's so much to read you can't pay attention to anything else.

If you chase two rabbits, you won't catch either one. *People can read or they can listen,* but they can't do both. As author Dave Crenshaw points out in his book *The Myth of Multitasking: How "Doing It All" Gets Nothing Done,* there is no such thing as true multitasking, only "switchtasking."[20] Loading your slide with text tells the audience to immediately begin reading. Reading is boring.

We want the audience to get your clear message right away and then get their eyes back on the road (meaning you). This means images and few words. It means drawing their attention to a purposeful point.

Aspect Ratio

Choose your slide size now—it can be a chore to change later!

Aspect ratio = screen proportions. This is one of the first decisions to make when designing a new slide deck. The two standards are 16:9 and 4:3.

Most TVs are 16:9, but many projector screens are still 4:3. My preference is usually still 4:3. First, I consider the images I will be using. Professional SLR cameras shoot in 3:2, which is closer to 4:3 than to 16:9. This means less cropping because the image I'm using is closer to the original size.

I have found that the original image might be nicely composed (more on that later), but it's hard to maintain this composition when trying to crop a 3:2 image into a wide 16:9 slide. It's often nice to have images that cover the entire screen. However, as long as your background is black, your audience likely won't notice the black bars outside the image, called letterboxing.

Some phones now allow you to choose the aspect ratio of your photographs, so consider this when taking photos for your presentations.

Forget about Templates

Set your slide master to a left-aligned text box with a font that you want to carry through your entire presentation, and select a *black background*. This doesn't mean that you should use a black background on every slide, but it will set you up with a canvas that's easier to work with than white.

A bright white background can be difficult to look at, especially in a dimly lit conference room. That glowing white rectangle can also be distracting and compete with you for attention. A darker background is often more subtle and is easier on the eyes.

The premade templates within PowerPoint look so tempting. It's easy to think, "Hey, someone's done all the work for me!" Do not be seduced. These are overused and will murder your creativity. They are a dressed-up version of the basic slide that begs you to fill it with bullet points instead of meaningful images.

You may want to choose a *background color* scheme that will unify your presentation. There are some nice template backgrounds available within PowerPoint. The problem is the popular ones tend to get used a lot, and some audience members may immediately recognize them as standard templates.

Another option is to search the internet for background images that you can size properly once and use throughout your presentation. A simple image search for "blue background," for example, will give you hundreds of great images. A subtle background graphic can be more appealing and interesting than a solid color. This will give your backgrounds a bit of texture without distracting the audience from the text.

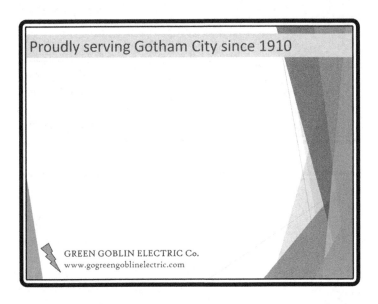

Some workplaces want you to use their *corporate standard* template for all presentations. They do this so that there is consistency across their media—the same branding, font, font size, color scheme, blah, blah, blah. Why would you want everything to be the same? How does your message stand out? Also, who is this for? If you work for the company, do you need to be reminded of that fact on every slide? Imagine sitting through a corporate training program over several months in which *every* slide is just like the last!

I say, "Fight the power!" I've had good success in going to the decision-makers on this issue and politely asking them the rationale behind their standard template. Most of them don't have an answer. That being said, if you're stuck using one, you'll just have to up your game in content and delivery.

Even for presentations outside your business, the audience knows who's speaking to them, so stop with the constant distracting brand reminder.

The only time that this might be appropriate is if you're using your presentation as an emailed PDF document. You don't know where this document will end up, and you want to ensure that everyone knows where it came from. The difference here is that it's used as a *document*—not a presentation.

Don't touch the transitions! No one is going to notice or care about how your slides change from one to another unless you give them a reason to. If you must, keep it super simple—this means *maybe* a quick fade of 0.5 seconds (dissolve in Keynote). Anything else—I'm talking to you, Shape, Wipe, and Blinds—distracts the audience and looks childish.

Pictures Are Better than Words

Get the highest *quality images* you can. Great images can be found all over the internet, including from free stock image websites. If you can't find what you're looking for, consider taking your own pictures.

Aim to make your images "full bleed." This means that the image covers the entire area of the screen. It's a printing term that means the print goes beyond the edge of where the sheet will be trimmed.

Some images will already be the perfect shape, but most will require some cropping. Use the *crop tool* to change the aspect ratio of your image to match your slide. Cropping an image will reduce the number of pixels you're able to display, which is why you should always start out with high-resolution images.

A great image may be sufficient on its own. However, consider adding a word or two to reinforce the message of the slide. This will mean adding text over top of your image. Play around with the color of both the text and the image until you find a balance. Often images have mixtures of light and dark colors, which makes it difficult to have the text stand out.

Consider using a solid color or semitransparent text box to give you the right backdrop to the text.

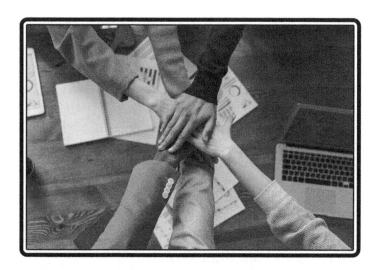

Avoid cheesy stock images. An image search for a term like "teamwork" will show you all kinds of clichéd, posed shots of culturally mixed, smiling, and beautiful employees huddled around a table. Don't take the bait! This smacks of bland corporate unoriginality. Instead consider other types of "teams" that will be more engaging or that will create an emotional response—think SWAT team, skydiving team, or pro sports team.

Go one step further and search for words adjacent to what you're looking for. Your message about teamwork might also be about trust … try a search for that. You've got to admit, this image of a Marine kissing his dog is far more powerful than the cringe-worthy corporate fist bump.

PowerPoint has powerful editing tools built in that are worth getting to know. A very handy one is *Remove Background*. Let's say you want to use the flowers from this image but not the background of the clouds. Removing the background makes it transparent. The leftover flowers can then be resized and repurposed with a new background.

Removing a background is easiest when what you're working with has defined edges that are easily distinguished. If the edge of what you're trying to cut out is blurry or very fine (like grass or hair) this can quickly turn into an exercise in frustration that might eventually produce a jagged-edged piece of crap. Another option is to search for images with transparent backgrounds where someone else has already done the work.

Slide Composition

"One of the most important elements of photography to understand is how the viewer's eye is drawn through the image. You may think that when you view a photograph you see the whole picture as one. In one sense this is true, as you can absorb much of an image in a millisecond. At the same

time, your eye moves through an image in a way
that you're usually completely unaware of."

—Rowan Sims, travel photographer[21]

You might be thinking, "Hey, I'm not a photographer, why should I care about this?" Maybe so, but since you are putting images up on a huge screen for an audience, it will serve you well to understand a few basic concepts of photography. With a bit of intention, we can craft where the viewer's eye will go and what they'll focus on.

The *rule of thirds* in composition is where an image is divided into thirds horizontally and vertically. The subject of the image is placed at the intersection of those dividing lines or along one of the lines.

Aligning a subject with these points creates more tension, energy, and interest in the composition than simply centering the subject. Photographers and designers sleep, eat, and breathe this rule. It's one of the reasons why the pictures from the wedding photographer are so much better than anyone else's.

When taking scenic shots, use the grid lines in your camera or phone and place the horizon line on one of the thirds. This will make for better pictures, keep the horizon nice and level, and give you a handy spot to put text in if you use it in a slide.

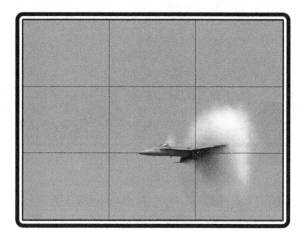

If we wanted to use this image of a jet, we can size the image down until it's on one of the intersecting points. Use the *Eyedropper* tool to match the slide background to the sky so it all looks seamless. Add some text in the negative space, and you're all set.

Let's say we want to use this image of a fighter pilot on the left. Placing the text across the top of the image would be ok, but not very dramatic. We could also try to cram it up in the top right corner. A better option is to crop the image to make room for text at the intersection. Again, it's important to use a high-resolution image so that when you crop it the result is still sharp.

In the slide on the left, the character has been placed along a ⅓ line with his face nicely at an intersection point. But … now he's looking off the page into nothingness. Typically, it's more appealing to have subjects facing into the image. If they're going to be looking out, it should be done with purpose. The slide on the right corrects for this.

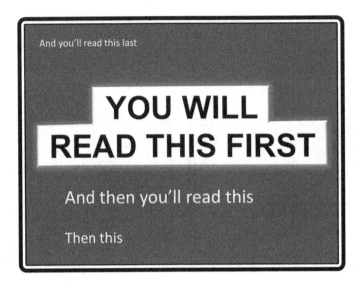

Pay attention to *where your eye goes* on a slide. People don't read a slide top down like they would a book. This can be difficult to accommodate when making the presentation, so give it some time, then go back and have a look with fresh eyes, and as always, have someone else give you feedback. Notice how your eye jumps around. This is also what makes things like page numbers and corporate branding in the corners so distracting. Every word should add to your message.

Our minds think in pictures and don't process words on a slide like they do when we're reading text. Here, the eye doesn't process the word "right" and instead subconsciously follows the bright arrows.

Bright Spots and Dark Spots

Notice where your eye automatically goes in the images above—are you drawn to the bright or dark spots first? If this is not what you want for your slide, then you may have to change out the image.

Where does your eye go in this picture? Likely first to the faces, then to the dark spot—the gloves on the slope. Those gloves are distracting and continually pull the eye away from the focus—the climbers.

Remove distractions whenever possible when taking a picture. This means composing the shot with purpose. Run your eye around the edge of the picture to hunt for "clutter"—like posts or trees in the background protruding from people's heads—and get rid of it. Fixing it might mean moving closer to your subject or changing your angle.

What other options do you have if you really want to use a particular picture?

1. Cropping can sometimes cut out the distracting item.
2. Put a text box or other item over it.
3. Cut the subject out and put it on another background.
4. Use software (like Adobe Photoshop, or free apps like Snapseed) to erase the distracting item with a healing tool.

The gloves were removed using the Snapseed healing tool. That's better!

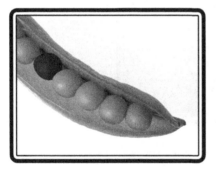

The human eye has evolved to spot and be attracted to bright colors—it might be a piece of fruit in a tree! Notice how even in a black and white image that your eye is drawn to the pea of a different shade (in this case the color version of the image has one red pea). This fact can be used to highlight certain words in your presentation to make them stand out. Here the words "like a war" stand out due to the thick font. The color version of this image also has the words in red while the rest of the image is in black and white.

Too much color can be distracting, so you may want to desaturate your image (like making it black and white) so that you can highlight a bit of text.

This is why portrait photographers often ask families not to wear bright colors—it distracts from skin-toned faces.

A note on color. The color you chose for your images and slides is important because it creates mood and helps to highlight important stuff. This book is printed in black and white which keeps printing costs down and makes it more accessible. The section about use of color that would have appeared here is available for free. Just go to www.kickasspresentationsbook.com.

Notice how the eye is naturally led into these images above. It would be counterproductive to crop them or put text over top of these lines.

Our eyes can't stand blurry things, and they'll try to focus until the image is sharp. Our eyes need something that's in focus to rest on. This is why photographers go to great lengths to create depth of field, such as in the image of the stormtrooper. Your eye knows right where to go. The same thing happens while panning with a moving subject. Next time you take a picture of a person, try putting your camera on Portrait mode to blur the background.

Take Your Slides from Good to Kickass

Now that you are armed with some extra knowledge, let's look at some common slide issues and how to improve on them:

Title: Is it necessary? We often confuse the "topic" of the slide with the *takeaway message*. Remember that this slide is for the audience, not for you. What do you want them to remember?

Too many words: The audience will immediately start to read ahead, which means they won't be listening to what you're saying.

Keep it simple and sleek. The words we removed from the slide can be said by the presenter and kept in the slide notes. In many rooms, even small ones, audience members can have a difficult time seeing the bottom of the slide, so try to *keep your takeaway message in the top half* (or at least not right along the bottom). By having fewer words on the slide, you can make the font size larger and easier for your audience to see.

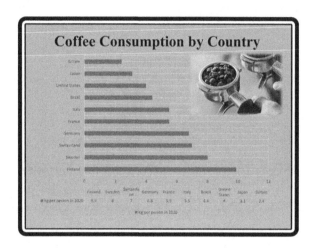

The audience doesn't want your data—they want *your conclusions*. What does this data mean, and why is it important to them?

Using data to support your message can be a good thing (and may even be necessary for your audience). When you look at this slide, what's your first impression? Most of the audience will be lost in trying to figure out what all this tiny data means.

Before using a chart of any kind, ask yourself what story you're trying to tell. Does this chart serve your purpose, or can you get the point across some other way?

This slide was created using the Insert Chart function in PowerPoint, which takes an Excel spreadsheet and converts it into a slide. Handy, but dangerous! This slide is very busy and doesn't highlight the takeaway message—in this case let's say we're highlighting the US data for a US audience. Even the text on the slide doesn't help us much. The heading is a title, not a takeaway. The picture just adds to the distraction and pulls the eye away from the chart.

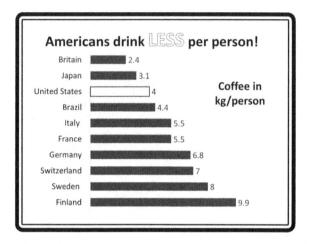

Here the US data is highlighted. Notice how your eye goes right to the outlier—the white bar. We've removed the distracting lines and extra info.

If it doesn't help you to tell the story or prove your point, get rid of it.

Define your takeaway message and put it up front.

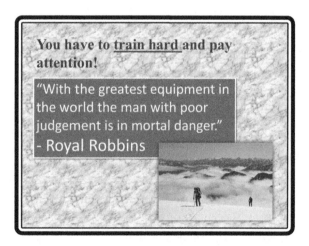

This is typical of an average slide—too many words in a busy background. If the takeaway message is the quote, then let's make sure it's more of the focus.

Now the important part—the quote—has been placed on top of the image.

Quoting someone who is wiser than you can be a great way to leverage their expertise and credibility. If you're going to use a quote, *memorize it.* When you get to where you need it, say it first and then display the words on the screen. This shows that you have command of the material. It stops you from reading off the screen and stops the audience from reading ahead of you.

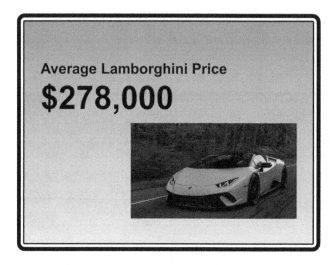

Ok, what is the takeaway message here? The average cost. The car is used to make the slide more interesting and to show what a Lambo looks like in case anyone's been trapped in a bunker since the 1960s. This is typical of many slides in that we simply put in some words and slap in an image. Also, I made up the number for demonstration purposes. Is this the actual price of a Lamborghini? I have no idea.

Avoid the collage! Collages are too busy, and the eye doesn't know where to go. Notice that some of the white text is very hard to see.

This image is pixilated, which is what happens when we take a thumbnail image with a low number of pixels and blow it up to fit the screen. Also notice that by keeping the grey-and-white gradient background that we've created letterboxing that will look like a grey stripe on the top of the image and a white bar below. These are distracting, so at minimum, the background should be changed to black.

Ok, we've made the background black and inserted the same image with a higher resolution. It's not terrible, but let's see if we can go full bleed.

Uh-oh! Instead of cropping the image we've stretched it to fit. The result is immediately noticeable and distracting—a chubby Lamborghini. PowerPoint allows you to crop an image to exact aspect ratios, so you don't have to guess.

Here it is cropped to 4:3 to fit the slide and eliminate the letterboxing.

Some images are trademarked and may even be protected by a watermark. My advice is that unless you're going to pay for the rights to the image, leave it alone and keep looking.

Let's stay with the Lambo theme and say we want to use this image but without the letterboxing.

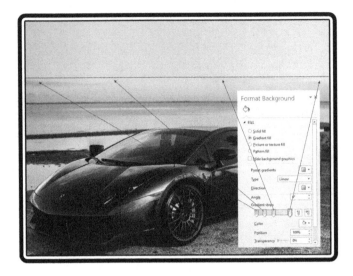

Instead of cropping the image to fit the screen (4:3), we've moved it to the bottom of the screen. The slide background has been changed to a gradient to match the sky by using the Eyedropper tool to sample the image in four spots. It's not perfect, but it will fool most people.

Here the image has been cropped to 4:3 so that it doesn't sit so low on the slide. Notice that the white text isn't easily distinguished from the background. One way to help correct this is to add a shadow to the text.

Another way to have the light-colored text contrast with the background is to fill in the text box with a darker color. Here it's been changed to black with a bit of a gradient fill. It's easier to read but overlaps with the top of the car in a weird way. Next, we've changed the text to black in Arial font (a common sans serif derived from Helvetica). It looks ok but isn't very imaginative.

Because *we* are the presentation and we'll be talking *with* the slide, do we really need the words "Average Lamborghini Price?" What's important here is the dollar amount.

In the slide on the left, we've used the font Comic Sans, which looks childish.

Fonts help to create the look and feel of your slides and serif fonts (like the one on the right) tend to communicate quality and authority. Let's dive deeper into the vast world of fonts.

Let's Talk about Text, Baby!

Fonts

Fonts go a long way to create a *mood* and personality for your slide and your whole presentation.

Your first choice will be between a serif and sans serif font.

Serif comes from the Dutch word *schreef*, meaning dash or line.[22] Serif fonts have the tiny dashes coming off the ends of the letters and often use thin and thicker strokes (like the *o* in Bodini). Historically, serif font has been used in printed text such as books, magazines, and newsletters as it helps the eye flow across the words, making the text easier to read. However, on a screen, especially a small one, it tends to have the effect of making words run together, so generally, sans serif fonts are preferable for slides.

If in doubt, avoid serif fonts. However, we shouldn't totally discount them. If you want to communicate *history*, *quality*, and *authority* (think Rolex) or to relay that your brand is *established* and *trustworthy*, then a serif font might be right for your slide.

All of these logos use a serif font to project a certain perception of quality.

Sans (French for "without") serif fonts are generally used in advertising and when there is less text.

All of these logos use Helvetica (at least as a base). This sans serif typeface was developed in 1957 by Swiss designers Max Miedinger and Eduard Hoffmann. Miedinger and Hoffmann set out to create a neutral typeface that was clear, easy to read, and could be used on a wide variety of signage.[23]

Script fonts look like cursive handwriting where the letters are connected. If you are going to use them, do it sparingly. They can be difficult to read, so use a large font size. Look to pair them with nonscript words and avoid full sentences. If they're not used effectively, they can be distracting.

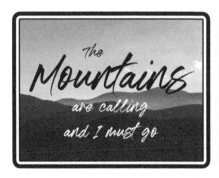 

Notice how in the mountains slide the font is stylish but might be difficult to read, especially at a glance. In the adventure slide, we pair some purposeful script to create mood and contrast it with some sans serif to make it easy to read.

Harrington
Matura
Old English
STENCIL
Cooper Black
Forte

For consistency, I recommend sticking with a sans serif base font for most of your slides. However, you can create interesting moods and looks by using some lesser-known fonts, such as those above. Draw attention to certain words or phrases and have them stand out by changing the color or font of that word. Combine this with using ALL CAPS to create a distinction.

Avoid using more than three fonts on a slide; otherwise, things start to look hectic and jumbled. Think about choosing a font, or font combinations, that will unify your deck.

Pay attention to advertisements, packaging, magazines, book covers, and other people's presentations. When you see a style you like, make note of it, and try it out in your own work.

These logos have been ironically rendered in the Comic Sans font. It makes everything look cartoonish and amateur. I can't see a reason to use it, but you should know it exists—mostly so that you can avoid it!

Comic Sans was created in 1995 by Vincent Connare of the Microsoft typography team. Connare created the font for a kids' computer tutorial called Microsoft Bob and told *The Guardian*, "When I loaded the CD a little dog came up. He talked in a speech balloon like you would get in a newspaper cartoon strip, but it was in the system font Times New Roman. Dogs don't talk in Times New Roman!"[24] Comic Sans was born and has become *the most polarizing font in history.*

According to a piece in The Cut, Comic Sans has been found to help people living with dyslexia.[25] That's one out of every six Canadians.[26] Apparently, the irregularity of the font and idiosyncrasy of the shapes and sizes of characters helps people with dyslexia to differentiate and identify letters and words.

PowerPoint offers a ton of great fonts to choose from, but you can also download a wide variety of others. This is handy because if you spot a font you want to use, such as from a company logo, chances are you can find it for download.

My caution with downloaded fonts is that the computer you're using to display your slideshow may not be compatible with that font. For example, you take your presentation on a flash drive to use on a computer supplied by the venue. If they're running an older version of PowerPoint or they don't have that font installed, you might see some glitches. When this happens, PowerPoint will choose a similar font, which could turn out to be a different size (for example, a 12-point font may be much larger in one font than another). This can cause text to be misaligned or even wrapped to another line.

I once had this happen to me 15 minutes before presenting to a room of 400 people! Luckily, I was there early enough to go through my deck and adjust all my text into a font that worked. I always recommend that you use your own laptop, but if you're on an unfamiliar computer, get there early and have a quick run through your deck to pick off these issues.

Lists and Bullet Points

A bullet point (•) is a symbol used to denote items in a list—or a way to slowly murder your audience. Synonymous with Death by PowerPoint, bullet points are often despised by audiences because they're about as fun as reading a grocery list. However, a few lists or points are sometimes required, so let's use some tricks to make it easier on the audience.

Use lists sparingly. It's not that audiences hate them; it's that they hate when there's a bunch of them. The hatred intensifies when the lists themselves are long and when they contain lots of words. To borrow an analogy from Andrew Ivey, lists work best as signposts to summarize what you've done and to show where you're going.[27] If the rest of your presentation is engaging and the lists are done well, the audience won't even notice them.

When you show an audience a slide with a full list on it, what do they do? They read ahead—which means they're not listening to you. To control this, one technique is to have the points appear as you talk about them. You can highlight the one you're speaking about and have previous items blend more with the background. This allows the audience to keep up when taking notes and prevents them from reading ahead.

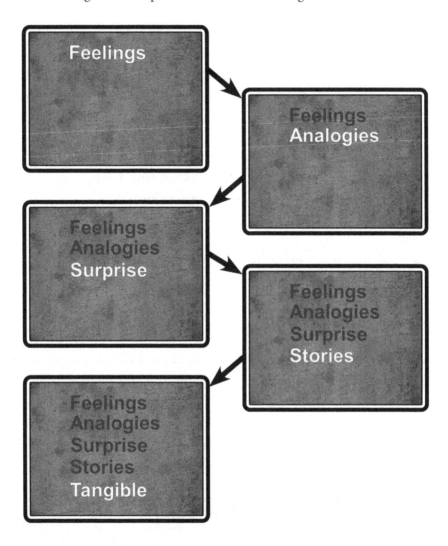

In this example, the list appears one item at a time over five slides. Start with your final slide and duplicate it once for each item on the screen. On the first slide, highlight your first point and delete the rest. In your second slide, highlight the second item, subdue the first item, and delete the rest. Carry this on for slides three, four, and five. The effect, when displayed for the audience, is an animated list where their eyes are drawn to the highlighted item.

Any time you're tempted to make a bullet list, consider whether presenting the points on their own slides could serve your purpose better.

If you must make a list, try to keep it to no more than six items—when there are seven or more items, people tend to categorize it as a long list and start to tune out. Some lists require numbers to denote a sequence. If this is the case, then go ahead. Otherwise get rid of the bullet or symbol in front of each item on the list.

> **"They say everything looks better with odd numbers of things. But sometimes I put even numbers—just to upset the critics."**
>
> —Bob Ross[28]

Now that you know some of "rules," go ahead and break them. The key is to create every slide with purpose.

Build a Kickass Intro Slide

Put extra effort into your intro slide. Think of it like the cover of a book. The text should be easy to read, even from the back of the room. This will be up while people enter the room, and it sets the expectation for what's about to happen. I can often predict how good a presentation is going to be based on the intro slide. If it's bland and unimaginative … you get the picture. Here are a couple of examples of intro slides I've used over the years:

Your Slides Are Not Their Notes!

I've lost track of how many presentations I've seen where the presenter hands out a thick stack of paper to each person. Each page has three slides on one side and some little lines next to each for notes. What does everyone immediately do? They thumb through the pack to see just how long and painful this will be. Stop it.

Your slides will likely be of limited value on their own. Why? Because they're mostly images and a few words.

Note—your speaker's notes are not your audience's notes! Your speaker's notes are for you. They let you keep track of important teaching points and references. They'll be super important if you're passing this presentation over to someone else. You can refer to them during the presentation, but hopefully you will have mastered your content and don't need them.

Research shows that retention is higher when people take their own notes. The simple act of writing something down means it'll stick in the mind longer. Come prepared with some extra paper and pens. It never ceases to amaze me that people show up to a presentation—especially a work training session—with nothing in their hands but a coffee.

Handouts

First, do you even need a handout? What do you expect your audience to do with it? It might be very important for them to refer to at some point in the future, but think about it carefully before you create and distribute a handout that will inevitably end up in the recycle bin. Instead, sending documents by email after the presentation will save paper and allow you to stay in contact. In the past I have followed up my presentation with a series of emails that remind my audience of a particular concept or technique and have asked them to take action and try them out.

My advice with physical handouts is to *wait until the end*. If you hand them out at the beginning, students feel like they don't have to take notes or sometimes even pay attention all. Why should they when they've got all the important stuff right there! You may also want to reveal concepts as you go, and having the answers in front of them may cheat them out of discussion opportunities and some valuable "A-ha!" moments.

What should be in your handout:

1. Some basics about the presentation, and your contact info
2. Important content and your takeaway messages
3. A few small, critical images or slides (if needed)
4. Your call to action
5. Resources

Slide Checklist

Now that you've built some slides, you can go through each one and make sure that it meets some basic criteria:

1. The takeaway message is the focus of the slide (one idea per slide).
2. Your image is sharp and helps explain your idea.
3. Text is
    a. Limited—do you even need any?
    b. Easy to see (in large font and in colors that stand out in the upper half of the slide).
    c. Not just the title—the text *is* your message.

    * You'll find all the checklists again at the end of the book.

Chapter Takeaways

1. Treat your slides like they are road signs.
2. Avoid the temptation of templates, and focus on your takeaway message.
3. Use the rule of thirds to compose beautiful slides.

4. Notice where your eye is drawn and remove distractions.

5. Remove anything that doesn't help tell your story or prove your point.

6. Fonts and color create mood, so choose them wisely.

7. Use lists sparingly.

8. Put extra effort into creating a great intro slide.

9. Your slides are not their notes—create purposeful handouts.

Exercises

Choose one slide that you currently use and run it through the slide checklist. Don't worry about the rest of the deck, just work on making this one slide better.

Take a picture with your phone and use the rule of thirds. Notice how your eye moves through the image. If you were going to use this image in a presentation, where would you put the text?

Chapter 4

MAKE YOUR MESSAGE STICK

You've got an idea in your head, and you want it to be in the heads of your students or audience members. Think back to Bloom's Taxonomy and that having your students remember the lesson material is the first level you're aiming for. They can't go on to apply what you've taught unless they can recall the information when needed and put it to use.

So, how do we make what we teach them stick in their minds? It can be tricky, but thankfully we can apply science and a few clever techniques.

What Makes Ideas Sticky—FASST

Sticky =
Feelings
Analogies
Surprise
Stories
Tangible

Let's start with the FASST checklist:

Hit 'Em in the Feels

Feelings stick with us. Think about some of the most emotional moments in your life—first day of school, first kiss, graduation, first date, first car, first wedding—I don't just mean happy feelings but also sadness, heartache, surprise, fright, wonder, outrage, and humor. So, how do we add emotion to our presentations?

Include faces: human faces, animal faces, faces drawn on things, or even emoji.

One glance at the face of this dog and you get an immediate sense of his loneliness. You can imagine that this poor guy has been left alone all day and can't wait for his owner to come through the door. This picture will be much stickier than just talking about a dog being left home alone.

Pictures elicit emotion while numbers are just numbers. Why do you think UNICEF uses the powerful image of one child as opposed to simply telling us that 350,000 children are without access to clean water? Our minds can't wrap themselves around large numbers, so the ad focuses on one child with a name, and it hits us right in the gut—and the wallet.

Let's take the example of plastic in our oceans. You can show all the stats you have, but if it's a change in behavior or a call to action that you want, then you must make the audience *feel* something.

Source: Surfrider; used by permission.

Check out this ad by the Surfrider Foundation. It's so much more visceral. You can imagine biting into this and the feeling it would have in your mouth.

Get your audience to use their imaginations. Keith Leech knows more about critical illness insurance than almost anyone on the planet. He's an excellent speaker and resource to many financial professionals. Critical illness insurance pays policy holders when they are diagnosed with things like cancer, heart attack, or stroke.

With today's medical technology, many people survive these events, but are unable to work for a time, often months. Rather than simply selling the idea that the policy will pay out, say, $100,000 cash, Leech asks prospective customers to imagine for themselves what they could do with that money.

Customers come up with images in their minds like, "I can take my family on a dream vacation to Europe," or "I can fly my sister in from Toronto to help look after the kids," or "I can go to Vegas and bet it all on black!" (Ok, maybe not that last one.) The point is it gets the customer involved in the process, and it's sticky because it engages their imagination and emotions.

One way to do this during a presentation is to have your audience close their eyes and visualize themselves in a situation. Whatever that situation is, make sure that the language you use creates the feeling you intend them to experience—be that good (like winning an Olympic Gold medal) or not so good (slipping in dog crap on the way to a job interview).

Use Analogies

In February of 1993, Jim Woolsey sat in front of a US Senate committee to give his confirmation testimony to become director of the CIA. The Cold War had just ended, and Woolsey was asked how he viewed the next decade of the post–Cold War environment.

Woolsey said, "We have slain a large dragon [referring to the Soviet Union]. But we live now in a jungle with a bewildering variety of snakes. And in many ways, the dragon was easier to keep track of."[29] The snakes he was referring to were a number of failed states, weak states, and nonstate actors. This analogy was easy to understand, and the picture it evoked made it memorable.

A kickass analogy makes new information familiar by emphasizing similarities between unrelated topics. The best analogies explain a connection by creating imagery in the audience's mind and help them to compare apples to oranges. (See what I did there?) When that imagery is novel, emotional, or surprising, it helps make the analogy even stickier. Here are some examples:

First, let's address the elephant in the room.

Worrying is like sitting in a rocking chair—it gives you something to do, but it doesn't get you anywhere.

You knock one down and the rest will fall like dominos.

Don't light yourself on fire to keep someone else warm.

That presentation was a soup sandwich.

Piece of pie, easy as cake.

When I think back to my own training, there are many analogies that have stuck with me through the years. For example, in trauma medicine, packing a wound is like building a beaver dam. The cloth fibers in gauze are the sticks, and they give the clotting blood (the mud) something to adhere to.

In an emergency a dense crowd doesn't flow like water; it flows like molasses.

Police officers should treat someone experiencing excited delirium syndrome as they would a rabid dog. Keep your distance, speak low and slow, and get your resources in place before you put your hands on them. (Couple this with a picture of an angry dog, and it becomes even stickier.)

Here's one from later in this very chapter: Easy learning is like writing in the sand. It's fun but it doesn't last long.

If you're writing your own analogy, start by thinking of things you can compare your idea to. What traits does it have? What is a key feature you want to highlight? What does the thing you're describing do? How should the analogy start? What happens in the end? The more familiar your new comparison is to your audience, the better. As you're building your presentation, keep your eye out for analogies that may be useful to you.

Avoid clichés! We've all heard them, and we're all guilty of using them (myself included). There are loads of overused and tired sayings that seem like they fit but certainly aren't sticky: nerves of steel; he sounds like a broken record; hit the ground running; a needle in a haystack; where the rubber meets the road; life is like a box of chocolates. Using expressions that everyone has heard a hundred times is like the waiter bringing your fajitas to the table after they've had a chance to cool. They'll still get eaten, but they won't have that sizzle.

Challenge your analogies. In a 2018 TEDx talk, author and presidential speech writer John Pollack tells of an analogy taken too far. He says that the United States accounts for one-quarter of all the world's prison population—over two million people. This is largely the result of a well-intentioned analogy made by the father of a murdered girl.

In the mid-1990s, the father led a ballot initiative in California requiring long sentences for offenders on their third conviction. It was called "Three Strikes and You're Out." Baseball is a fair game where everyone plays by the same rules. This tough-on-crime analogy also appears, on the surface, to be fair for everyone and speaks to individual accountability. It was adopted by California, and many other states followed suit, taking plenty of career criminals off the street.

The unintended consequence was that it completely hamstrung judges. They could no longer use their discretion in sentencing, and as a result, many people were locked up for 25 years to life for minor offenses, like shoplifting. This has destroyed thousands of lives and costs taxpayers billions each year.

Baseball provides many useful analogies. Pollack says, "The problem is not that 'Three Strikes and You're Out' oversimplifies things, because all analogies simplify things, that's what they're supposed to do. It's that the emotional appeal 'baseball is fair' distracted millions and millions of voters from more relevant disqualifying differences between the game of baseball and criminal justice."[30]

Our social media streams are full of analogy memes made by those on both sides of controversial issues. Unrelated topics are used in an attempt to persuade, regardless of how misleading or ridiculous the argument might be when looked at with a critical eye. Gun control is compared to drunk driving, and COVID masks to diapers. These issues may share some similarities, but they are not the same in most respects. Though they might be fun and convenient, they are often incomplete.

Take a close look at your analogies, and ask yourself if what you've chosen is correct, clear, and unoffensive. That way you don't end up like Homer Simpson trying to impart some wisdom on Bart: "Actually, a woman is more like a beer. They smell good; they look good, you'd step over your own mother just to get one."[31]

As always, run everything by someone you trust. A new analogy is like a dollar-store pregnancy test. It might be accurate, but you'd better get a second opinion.

Surprise Them

It was no different from the start to any other class in my first year as a university criminal justice student. This room was smaller than most, like a high school class, with about thirty desks. But no sooner had the professor opened her mouth when what seemed like all hell broke loose.

One male student a couple of rows in front of me jumped up and started screaming at another guy, something about sleeping with his girlfriend. The other student pulled out a small cap gun and fired off a few bangs at his accuser, who fell dramatically, crashing into desks and chairs on his way to the floor. Both men then sprinted out of the classroom—one out the back door and one out the front. The whole interaction took less than 10 seconds. What the hell was that? We all sat there, frozen and gobsmacked.

The prof broke the silence: "Everyone take out a blank sheet of paper." We were to record everything we could remember: What was each man wearing? How would we describe each man? What, exactly, was said by each? What type of gun did the shooter have? What hand was he holding it in? How many shots were fired? What door did each man leave by?

Predictably, we all had a hard time with the specifics. The prof then let students talk in small groups about what we saw to see if we could remember more together. A woman in my group said, "The shooter had on jeans, I'm sure of it!" Maybe the shooter had been wearing jeans. I wasn't paying particular attention, but ok, let's go with that.

This was an exercise designed to show how poor eyewitness testimony could be and how letting witnesses talk with each other could distort their memory. A surprising lesson? Absolutely. So surprising that it has stuck with me decades later.

There are several ways that we can manufacture surprise in our audience:

Reveal a gap in their knowledge by posing a question—especially to which there is a surprising answer—but hold off on revealing what that answer is. You could also present them with a scenario and ask them to predict how it will end.

This forces the students to roll the question around in their minds and try to solve the mystery. It forces them to dig into the lessons from their past experiences and keeps them engaged while you provide the explanation. The answer that fills the gap will be stickier than if you had simply given it to them.

Break their guessing machine. Movies like *Seven, The Sixth Sense, Fight Club,* and *The Usual Suspects* are memorable because we all love a good plot-twist ending. These stories are stickier than other movies because our expectations are violated with a surprise. You might not remember the details of the film, but that ending stays with you.

A subject I most enjoyed teaching to new police officers was how to talk to people. One of the first viral police dashcam videos, from 1992, featured Maine State Trooper Stephen Murray. The burly trooper in his Smokey the Bear hat conducts a traffic stop on a motorist who flips out on him and screams in his face. He even grabs the ticket from the trooper's hand, tears it up, and throws the bits out of the window. The trooper calmly tells the man that he had better pick up the papers, or he will be cited for littering. The old man mutters as he picks up the confetti and then slams his door before driving off in a huff.[32] New recruits are quick to point out how calm and professional the trooper stayed in the face of the man's tantrum.

After several days of instruction and exercises on active listening, persuasion techniques, and rapport building, the recruits are shown the video again. Now they view it in a much different light. They pick up immediately on the slightly sarcastic tone in the trooper's voice and see where the trooper missed opportunities to show empathy and potentially turn the interaction around. *Their guessing machines failed and revealed a gap in their knowledge.* This change in their point of view is far more powerful and memorable than simply playing the video once and pointing out how the trooper could have done better.

And finally, in 2009 this small-batch organic breakfast cereal was launched in British Columbia. Originally called Hapi Food, they changed its name when one of their first customers tasted it and declared, "Holy Crap!" Surprising and sticky? Yes. Sales jumped 1,000%.[33]

Tell Stories

Stories can be a presenter's most effective weapon. We all love a good story, and we also tend to remember them. Your story may be about *you*, but it's for *them*. The key is to tell relevant stories that *reinforce your message*. How do we make sure it's relevant? According to research by storytelling expert Kindra Hall in her incredible book *Stories That Stick*, you should be asking yourself these questions:[34]

1. Who is my audience?
2. What do I want them to think, feel, know, or do?

Great storytelling isn't complicated. Hall identifies these four essential ingredients to any great story:[35]

An identifiable character. We don't need a hero—we need someone we care about and can connect with. It has to be a person, so not a police department, a company, a group of people, a product, or a thing (unless you turn it into a person, like the Kool-Aid Man or Planters' Mr. Peanut).

Authentic emotion. This can be as simple as frustration or wonder. The emotion does not refer to what the audience feels but to what the character experiences (even if the character is you). What can help the emotion to come through is acting out what the characters were thinking or saying. Here's an example: "I walked fast to get there and figured I'd be late," (no emotion) versus, "As I hopped out of the car, I checked my watch (actually checking your watch): 10:58! Crap! I'm gonna be late for sure!" (Breathing out a big breath.)

A significant moment. Identify a specific point in space, time, or circumstances. If our story is a map of a city, this is where we zoom in to a particular spot.

Imagine someone asked you about your experience at a fair. You could say, "It was fun. We hit a bunch of rides and ate cotton candy." Not very interesting. Instead, look to zoom in on one moment. "We were cruising the midway, and then Steve and I dared each other to go on the Slingshot. When the dude clipped me into the five-point safety harness, I looked over at Steve—his face was white! His eyes were closed, and he was doing some deep breathing! I giggled until we launched, and then I wasn't laughing anymore … The thrust sucked me right into my seat, and all I could do was pray that our little pod was still attached to the ride."

Zooming in aids what Hall calls the "co-creative process," where listeners actively engage in visualizing the story in their own minds—which makes the story stick.

Specific details. Specific and fine details engage the audience's imagination and pull them deeper into the story.

For example, you could say, "We took a rest from our walk and listened to the birds sing." But adding a few details makes it even more engaging, "We took a rest on the sunny trunk of a fallen poplar tree and listened to a blue jay's call that sounded like, 'Thief! Thief! Thief!' "

Instead of saying, "She went back to school and graduated university in her sixties," be specific and say, "She went back to school and graduated university at the age of sixty-seven."

Including vivid and specific details helps your audience visualize the event you're describing and adds tiny hooks that their minds can latch on to. Instead of, "I wasted the day watching cartoons," try, "I wasted the day watching twelve episodes of *SpongeBob SquarePants.*"

You don't need to absolutely load your story with details, but be purposeful about including some.

In the movie *Pulp Fiction*, there's a famous flashback scene where Capt. Koons, played by Christopher Walken, goes in his Air Force dress blue uniform to visit a young boy named Butch Coolidge and present him with a small gold watch. Capt. Koons' story starts out like this:

> This watch I got here was first purchased by your great-grand-father during the First World War. It was bought in a little

general store in Knoxville, Tennessee. Made by the first company to ever make wrist watches (…) It was bought by Private
Doughboy Erine Coolidge on the day he set sail for Paris.
This was your great-grandfather's war watch and he wore it
every day he was in that war. When he had done his duty, he
went home to your great-grandmother, took the watch off,
put it in an ol' coffee can. And in that can it stayed 'til your
granddad, Dane Coolidge, was called upon by his country to
go overseas and fight the Germans once again. This time they
called it World War Two.[36]

The story gets much more interesting as it goes, and if you haven't seen it, I
encourage you to check it out. The story pulls you in because of the specific details it offers. It also sets the stage for when an adult Butch, played by
Bruce Willis, risks his life to get the watch back.

How sticky are the safety briefings on a commercial aircraft? Look around
on your next flight, and you'll likely see people doing everything *but* paying attention to the demonstration. One standard line in that briefing may
be something along the lines of, "If we experience a sudden change in
cabin pressure, an oxygen mask will automatically drop from the panel
above you. Please put on your own mask before assisting others." You can
imagine doing this, but when tragedy strikes, will you?

According to research conducted by the Royal Australian Air Force, at an
altitude of 40,000 feet passengers may have a mere 15 seconds of "useful
consciousness" after rapid decompression.[37] Now picture how many of
your precious seconds you would use up trying to fit a mask on a screaming toddler. This one little detail makes the whole message much stickier.

Coming up with personal stories can be harder than you think. Sometimes
we recognize a situation as something that could be crafted into story—if
only we can remember it. The same goes with comedians and recognizing something that could be the kernel of a joke. At the time it's easy to
think, "Oh, I'll remember this." Chances are your memory sucks as badly

as mine, and within an hour, if you have nowhere to put it, that idea will be lost forever. Create a *notepad on your phone* where you can jot these things down in the moment. The thought might not turn into anything, but at least you've captured it.

Where can you find stories? Everyone's got a ton of them if you know how to ask the right questions. When mining others for their stories, focus your open-ended questions on *people*, *places*, and *things*.

Have you ever been put on the spot by someone asking you a vague question like, "So, what's it like to live in Colorado?" Or, "Tell me about working at a hospital." This makes it tough to pull out an actual story. It's happened to me so many times as a police officer. I'd be at a BBQ, and someone would ask, "So what's it like to be cop?"

"Uh … I don't know, good I guess?" Guh! Between their wide-open question and my unprepared, slack-jawed answer, this conversation isn't going anywhere. I have a ton of great stories, but this question doesn't lead my mind to any of them.

When it's your turn to ask the questions, you can get straight to someone's kickass stories by being specific:

"What was your first day like as a teacher?"

"What was your favorite food experience on that cruise?"

"Who was your boss at IBM? What were they like?"

"Tell me about what it was like the first time you came under fire in Afghanistan."

"What's something you learned in prison that surprised you?"

Stories are sparked easily when we can relate them to items. For example, "Tell me about how you acquired this cool sculpture." "What did it feel like when you got your very first motorcycle?" "What was the craziest thing you ever found while cleaning a hotel room?"

Make It Tangible

In 1990, Elizabeth Newton earned a PhD in psychology from Stanford by studying a simple game in which she assigned people to one of two roles: "tappers" or "listeners."[38] Tappers received a list of 25 well-known songs, such as "Happy Birthday." Each tapper was asked to pick a song and tap out the rhythm to a listener by knocking on a table. The listener's job was to guess the song, based on the rhythm being tapped.

The tappers were asked to estimate the likelihood of the listeners guessing the song. Half the time the tappers thought for sure the listeners would guess correctly. However, once the exercise started, the listeners had a much harder time, guessing correctly only one time in 40. The tappers couldn't believe it—these songs were so easy!

What the heck was going on here? Newton had bestowed the tappers with the *curse of knowledge*. While the listeners just heard a bunch of tapping, the tappers had the song playing in their head. For the tappers, it was almost impossible for them to understand how difficult the task was from the listeners' perspective.

When we know something really well, it's hard to imagine what it's like not to know it. We become "cursed" with knowledge, and it causes us to think that we are better communicators than we really are.

Many board games and TV game shows simply give one player this curse and, inevitably, hilarity ensues—think Charades, Pictionary, or Taboo.

This is a fun exercise that I like to do with students. I pair them up, then take one-half of each pair out of the room with me and explain the drill. They pick a song that everyone knows and then head back in to tap it out for the listeners. Here are some songs that everyone should know: "All

Star" by Smashmouth, "Don't Stop Believin' " by Journey, and "Livin' on a Prayer" by Bon Jovi. Pro tip: don't use "Twinkle, Twinkle, Little Star" or the alphabet song … they have the same tune. (Go ahead, I'll wait.)

How Do We Beat the Curse of Knowledge?

First, understand that it exists and actively look for it in your own presentations. Put yourself in the shoes of your audience and look at your material from their level of knowledge and experience.

Second, have someone from outside of your industry or company sit through your presentation. They will be very quick to point out all the inside jargon and TLAs (three letter acronyms) that you use as a second language but make no sense to them. Every industry and hobby have their own language, and everyone seems to think that theirs is the worst!

Third, make sure your audience knows that they are free to ask questions throughout your presentation. If you are asked to provide a better explanation of something, that's a clue to do it differently next time. Remember, you want your audience to leave feeling smarter—not dumber.

Fourth, use simple and tangible language.

For example, in August of 2015, massive swaths of coastal forests in Washington State were on fire. The plume of smoke drifted north and east over the Rocky Mountains, blanketing almost the entire province of Alberta. You could see the heavy smoke in the air and taste the ash on your tongue. Sooty gray dust settled over everything.

Environment Canada advised everyone to stay indoors and to avoid exercising outside. Why? Because levels of fine particulate matter were at 170 micrograms per cubic meter! Um, ok? What does 170 micrograms mean? For comparison they said that a bad air-quality day is normally around 30–40 micrograms. Interesting for scientists, but not sticky for the public.

Thankfully, they changed their messaging to something much more tangible and relatable: Breathing outside for 24 hours is the equivalent of being in a car with a smoker for four hours.[39] Much stickier. We can imagine being a child trapped in a car full of smokers. Many of us were once that kid!

One way to be tangible is to *keep things simple*. Present just *one idea per slide*. Remember, slides are free, so there's no need to cram ideas and content together.

> "Complexity is your enemy. Any fool
> can make something complicated. It
> is hard to keep things simple."
>
> —Richard Branson[40]

Picture Superiority

Here is a little exercise: Don't think of a Jeep. Do not imagine what color it is, if it has a top or not, and certainly don't think about how chubby the tires are. This is nearly impossible to do. We think in pictures. What's better than describing the image you want your audience to have in their minds? Showing them!

Research on this topic as far back as the 1970s clearly shows that *memory is more robust when subjects see an image* compared to just hearing the word.[41] Add text to that image, and we get an even bigger memory boost. Check out this picture of a wasp. We can all imagine one, but there's something visceral about just seeing the image. If the word "wasp" is important for the audience to remember, then consider putting it on the slide as well.

Advertisers know this, which is why so many billboards have pictures on them and only a few words—they're not crammed with forgettable text. We don't want any old image; we want one that is relevant and reinforces the takeaway message.

Make large numbers visual. Our minds have a hard time grasping large numbers. Whenever you have to present a large number, think about explaining it in a different way. Draw an analogy or compare it to something that the audience can visualize.

If over the course of one summer you drove 6,600 km (4,100 miles) while delivering pizza, one way to make it more tangible would be to say that it's the equivalent of driving from Chicago to Los Angeles and back—and then show that route on a map.

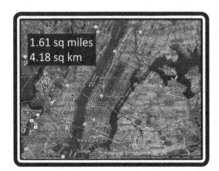 

If there are 30 thousand Starbucks locations worldwide,[42] and if the average Starbucks location is 1,500 sq feet (for a small one), the total area of Starbucks would take up 4.18 sq km or 1.61 sq miles or 1,033 acres[43]— larger than the size of New York's Central Park (which is 843 acres).[44]

This creates a sticky visual, provided that your audience is familiar with Central Park.

The best evidence rule. Law enforcement officers are taught to bring the best evidence to court. Why describe a gun when you can show a picture of it, and why show a picture when you can bring in the real thing for the judge and jury to see? Bringing in a prop and allowing students to hold it in their own hands is more tangible and engages more of the senses.

If you apply the five FASST techniques, you can guarantee that your presentation will be more memorable. Now, let's look at what the science tells us about memory and learning.

Memory and Learning

Hitting a pro fastball is one of the hardest things to do in sports. Batters have only a fraction of a second to determine the speed of the ball and where it will be in space, then start their swing to meet the ball and connect solidly.

In their best-selling book, *Make It Stick: The Science of Successful Learning*, authors Peter Brown, Henry Roediger, and Mark McDaniel tell the story of a study conducted with baseball players at California Polytechnic State University in San Luis Obispo.[45]

Players were divided into two groups, each of which were at bat for the same number and type of pitches: 15 fastballs, 15 curveballs, and 15 changeups. A changeup is a common off-speed pitch, usually thrown to look like a fastball but arriving much more slowly to the plate. Its reduced speed coupled with its deceptive delivery is meant to confuse the batter's timing and often results in the batter swinging early.

One group had 15 of the same pitch come at them and then 15 of the next. The second group had the same number of pitches but in random order. They did this same practice twice a week for six weeks.

When a batting test was conducted immediately afterward, the group that had all of one type of pitch did better than the randomized group. However, in subsequent practices and real games, the randomized group performed better. Why?

It has to do with retrieval.

Both groups had to learn what the start of each type of pitch looked like and make a mental model of what the pitcher's body was doing and what the ball was doing in the air. The group that got the same pitch thrown at them over and over could put their minds on autopilot because they knew what was coming. The randomized group had to work a little harder for each pitch because they didn't know what was coming at them. With every pitch they would have to retrieve what they knew about each from memory and put it into action.

Learning = Storage + Retrieval

Have you ever been asked a question to which you answered, "I don't know," only to hear the answer and remember that you did know? You had the information in storage, just not the ability to retrieve it. This happens to me all the time watching *Jeopardy* on TV. "Dammit! I knew that!"

Imagine that your mind is like a giant, dense forest. When you learn something new, it gets placed on the ground somewhere in that forest. Every time you need that piece of info, you have to find your way back to it. The more often we go to get it, the easier it is to find. Eventually we know the new information or skill so well that we've beaten a path right to it. This is what was meant by French essayist Joseph Joubert when he said, "To teach is to learn twice."[46]

Many students prefer multiple choice (or as some called them, "multiple guess") over short-answer tests. Of course they do! Multiple choice tests are easier because they only involve *recognition* and not *retrieval*.

How practice works. The path that gets beaten down to the information is due to a process called myelination. Myelin is a fatty substance that acts as insulation around the neural pathways in the brain, a little like electrical tape wrapped around a wire. The thicker the electrical tape, the less likely the energy flowing along the wire is to jump off onto another path. In the same way, the thicker the layer of myelin, the more robust the neural pathways and the more embedded the skill or knowledge will be.

Myelination happens through practice and repetition. Eventually, you've done something so many times that it seems like you can do it on autopilot—riding a bike, playing a song on the guitar, or driving a car. This is where the term "muscle memory" comes from, though it has little to do with your muscles. What was once difficult and awkward has become a programmed habit that runs in the background while we do other things. Don't believe me? Try brushing your teeth tonight with your nondominant hand.

How not to study. When I was at university, I studied as I assumed most others did. I read and reread the textbooks and my notes from class. I highlighted what I thought was the important stuff and spent more time on it. Eventually it all started to look familiar, and I figured I had it.

I would "cram" for a couple of days leading up to the test until I felt like I had a grip on the material and then walk into class and dump it all over the page. "Nailed it!" I passed my courses, but I don't think I've retained much. This is because I wasn't doing any retrieval. Familiarity gives us merely *the illusion of mastery*.

Learning is deeper and more durable when it's *effortful*.

So how can we learn and retain things better and have our students do the same? The answer is through *effortful retrieval*. The more often we go into our memory to find that piece of information, the more robust our ability to do it becomes. Learning comes from *the struggle*. If it's casual and easy, it will not be retained in the long term.

Thankfully, we can change how we study. We know that simply reading the same information over and over doesn't help. We need to find ways to force ourselves to retrieve the information. That means using *flash cards* or having someone else ask you the questions without having the answer available.

Increase Learning through Teaching

How would you go about learning a new skill, like memorizing facts or learning how to run some new software? Most people would review the basics, complete some practice exercises, reach an acceptable level of proficiency, and then move on to the next topic or section. This is called block practicing.

Block practice is when you focus on learning one skill at a time. You practice one problem type, topic, or physical skill repetitively for a period of time and then you move on to another. If you want to learn skills A, B, and C, then a block practice session would look something like AAABBBCCC.

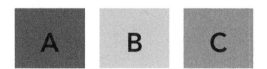

Interleaved practice, on the other hand, involves working on multiple skills in parallel. Interleaved practice sessions would look like ABCABCABC (in series) or ACBABCBAC (randomized). The only constraint is that you can't work on the same type of problem back-to-back. Now, when the learner returns to the first topic, they must start by recalling its content.

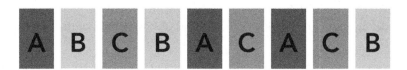

Many studies have been done around the effects of block vs. interleaved practice. Just as in the experiment with the baseball players, the results are predictable. Blocked practice will help students perform well immediately afterward, but those using interleaved practice get far better results in the days and weeks following the lesson—when they actually need it! Why? It's all about retrieval. Block practice is a bit like setting your car on cruise control—it's easy. Easy learning is like *writing in the sand*. It's fun but it doesn't last long.

Interleaved practice achieves the greatest results when learning physical skills and when problems can be quickly understood. Students must have some baseline knowledge, or the interleaving may just add to the confusion. Some research suggests that interleaving may not be helpful for complex subjects, like learning a new language.

Robust learning is obtained through stop-and-go lessons. This forces the learner to search for where the lesson has been stored in their mind. The harder you have to work to retrieve a memory, the better it will be retained. This can be difficult and frustrating for both the students and the instructor—you just get going on one subject, and the students are starting to pick it up, and then you switch to something else. Students won't always appreciate this, so tell them *what* you're doing and *why*. Experiment with the format, and see what works for you.

Spaced Learning

What's going to get you better prepared for running a 5k race: running once a week for two hours straight or four times a week for 30 minutes? You're doing the same amount of work, but your muscles need a break to recover. Your mind is no different. Spacing out your lessons allows for some absorption time. The same goes for practice and learning … *spacing things out allows for a little bit of forgetting*, which in turn makes retrieval harder and more frustrating, which boosts the robustness of the learning.

I get it. Spaced learning isn't always possible, especially in the context of a one-time presentation. Giving a series of presentations may give you the opportunity to have students recall some of the concepts from a previous session. The same applies to studying or learning a new skill. Break your own learning up into shorter chunks of time to make the retrieval a bit tougher.

Spacing the learning can be very challenging, even if you teach in a setting like a law enforcement academy. Block training is way easier because you can get everything done in one period of time, with the same instructors, the same facility, and the same students.

For example, in the academy where I taught, we did all our driver training in the same week as it was easy to schedule for the recruits and the staff. Spreading that out over a few weeks or months would be cumbersome. If you are not able to space the learning out over many sessions, look for opportunities in the time you *do* have to use spaced and interleaved teaching.

The Importance of Context

Have you ever noticed that you do better on a test if it's taken in the same room where the material was learned? The art on the walls, the color of the tables, and even the lighting levels are stored in the subconscious along with the information and can subtly help you with retrieval.

If we expect students to be able to retrieve information or skills under a certain context, it helps to have them learn under a similar context. This gives the mind more hooks on which to hang the information and provides retrieval cues for that environment.

For example, divers who are given a list of words to memorize under water have better retrieval when tested under water than on dry land. Even having the same music playing as when the lesson was learned will help in retrieval.

Consider the environment your students will be in when expected to recall information.

When I was training police recruits in arrest-control tactics, we would start in a large, well-lit room with padded floors and walls. This is a safe place to start, but in my entire policing career, I never arrested anyone in a room like that. Students get the basics down, and then we move them into small rooms, hallways, doorways, and even out on the street to between vehicles.

Our training facility was full of fake foam furniture and props and gave us the option to change the noise level and the lighting. This allowed recruits to practice their skills in what actually looked like a bedroom or a restaurant to mimic the environments they will likely find themselves in.

If they'll be required to recall in varied settings, then vary the settings they learn in.

Think about the information and skills you teach and about how to build context around what will serve your students when they need to retrieve those lessons.

Increase Learning through Testing

> "We act as if a test is the equivalent to putting a dipstick into a student's mind to see how much they know. The act of testing changes and strengthens memory."
> —Peter Brown, Mark McDaniel, and Henry Roediger[47]

In *Make it Stick*, the authors tell the story of Professor Andrew Sobel, who teaches political economics at Washington University in St. Louis. This is an auditorium lecture-style course, and he noticed that attendance always dwindled as the semester went on.

He heard about the learning effects of testing and decided to replace the midterm and final exams with nine scheduled quizzes. Each quiz contained information from *the entire course to that point* and not just what was taught the previous week. Each was worth less than 10% of their final grade, and if students missed one, it was their own fault.

As a result, the kids loved it, and grades went up along with the quality of in-class discussion and written work. Through this testing students were continually forced to retrieve the information they'd learned.

Sobel said, "As good a teacher as I think I am, my teaching is only a **component** of their learning, and how I structure it has a lot do with it, maybe even more."[48]

How can you build this into your own kickass teaching?

1. Incorporate fill-in-the-blank and short-answer questions in tests and quizzes. This forces students to retrieve the information as opposed to just recognizing the answer in a multiple-choice question.
2. Incorporate reviews and games that require retrieval. Some good options can be found in chapter 9.
3. At the start of the day on multiday training courses, have students recall something that they learned the day before and give an example of how they plan to use it. You can also ask them direct questions about material from previous sessions. However, from my own experience, I should warn you to prepare to be disappointed. It's not uncommon for students to sit dumbfounded as if they've never seen this stuff before. All the more reason for the review.

Opportunities for retrieval can also be done in class, even during a short presentation.

1. The pop quiz—have students put away their notes and answer some questions about what they've already learned in that presentation.
2. The teach-back—have students explain a concept from the presentation in their own words to a partner. A bonus is to have them describe when and how they would use this information.
3. The quick review—anyone who has spent even a hot minute in the Canadian Forces will be familiar with this statement: "If you

don't have any questions, then I have some for you." This is the standard line to start the end-of-class review. All you do is ask the class some questions about the key concepts you just went over.

Chapter Takeaways

1. Help make your message stick by using feelings, analogies, surprise, stories, and tangible language.
2. To truly learn something, we must not only store it in our minds but be able to retrieve it when we need it.
3. Learning is more robust when it comes from effortful retrieval. Instructors can create this through stop-and-go practice, interleaved practice, and spaced learning.
4. In-class quizzes, teach-backs, and reviews all help students to retain what they learned.

Exercise

Open up a presentation and pick one key takeaway. What analogies do you currently use to make it stickier? Find an important concept and write or find a fun analogy that will help your audience to remember it when they need it.

Think about a current presentation and how can you build the opportunity for effortful retrieval through a quick, no-steaks pop quiz. Write out the quiz and your plan to use it.

Chapter 5

YOU'VE GOT TO BE JOKING!

Imagine that you walk into a training session as a student and are faced with two identical presentations. The only difference is that in one session you'll have a few laughs and in the other you won't. You'd pick the one with laughs every time—and so would your audience.

Humor brings good feelings, and *feelings connect us with our audience*. Not only that, but according to the American Psychological Association, "a growing body of research suggests that, when used effectively, classroom comedy can improve student performance by reducing anxiety, boosting participation and increasing students' motivation to focus on the material."[49] Humor is good for everyone, and it also *increases your likability and persuasiveness* as a presenter—so let's make it happen!

I know what you're thinking. "But I'm not funny." When we think of funny people, our minds tend to go to comedians, actors, and your one goofball friend who just cracks people up. *Ask for help from someone who is funny*. Find a person who you know has a great instinct for humor, and get them to go over your presentation with you.

Pay attention to what you find funny and how you joke with friends. If you love dry sarcasm, start with that. Maybe your forte is corny Dad-joke puns—cool. We may not all be hilarious, but we can *learn the formula* for what makes something funny.

The idea is to build your presentation and then, as author and comedy coach Judy Carter advises, give it some "comedy polish." [50] Remember that this is a presentation, not a stand-up comedy show. We don't need to have the audience rolling on the floor. Most professional comedians can't do that, and their *only* goal is to make the audience laugh. They're not trying to persuade, educate, or empower anyone.

Comedians go for big laughs and lots of them. A comic's set can even be broken down into LPM, or laughs per minute. Thankfully, you don't have to do this. We are going for *smiles* and the odd laugh. Work on making your presentation *fun*, and you're already way ahead of the pack.

I began my comedy career on a dare on my 40th birthday. I always envied stand-up comics, but I was too scared and lazy to try it out. Since that time, I've written jokes and performed at all kinds of venues in three countries, from luxury hotels to dive bars and comedy clubs to coffee shops.

Doing stand-up forced me to take a deep dive into what's funny and why. It forced me to write down exactly what I was going say, try it out on a live audience, and tweak it at future performances. When you're a comedian or as a presenter, the feedback you get from the audience on humor is immediate and genuine. If you get no feedback—that's also feedback.

"If people like the performer, then you've got 80% of it made."

—Johnny Carson[51]

Getting to know your audience members is a great way to build rapport and increase engagement. One of my favorite introduction techniques is to have each of them tell me one interesting thing about themselves. I'm not looking for their deepest secrets (this isn't therapy!) ... just something to get the conversation going, like a memorable holiday, an odd hobby, or a quirky pet. Some presentations won't allow for this, but it's worthwhile if you have the time.

Let's say you're in a classroom delivering a one-day workshop. Look to carve out 20 minutes at the beginning to get to know your audience through introductions or an ice-breaker. This will allow you to "spritz" (banter a bit) with the audience, to link your messages to their experience, and to make call back jokes later in your talk.

On top of introductions, it helps for them to have *name cards*. I just get students to make these with a folded piece of paper. This allows you to personalize your interactions by *using their names* and is much easier than relying on your memory.

Know your audience. I shouldn't have to say this, but I will. There is no quicker way to lose an audience, your credibility, or maybe even your job, than by telling a joke that rubs people the wrong way—trust me I've been there! If you are not sure about a joke, then don't use it. You're better off keeping it clean and getting a few smiles than to have most of the audience rolling on the floor but learn that you've deeply offended a few people. You don't want anyone walking out or writing your boss an all-caps email. If you think it might offend, leave it out.

Use Funny Words

"Wriggly, Squiffy, Lummox, and Boobs: What Makes Some Words Funny?" This is the title of a paper by University of Alberta professors Chris Westbury and Geoff Wallis for the *Journal of Experimental Psychology*. Here are the top 10 funniest English words, according to the research: Upchuck, bubby, boff, wriggly, yaps, giggle, cooch, guffaw, puffball, and jiggly. The study found that the hard *K* sound and the 'oo' (as in 'loot') were more likely to occur in funny words.[52]

Hard consonants stick in the ear. Look to use words with sounds like *K*, *D*, *P*, and *T*. Go ahead and think of a few of your favorite swear words. I bet most contain hard consonants! Words like jack, pickle, chicken, and gutter are fun to say. Many successful companies have used this to their advantage, such as Coca-Cola, IKEA, and Spanx. The hard consonants in "Kleenex" were likely a factor in it becoming what we now call all brands of facial tissue.

When the Taser was introduced to my police department in the mid-2000s, we did our best to encourage officers to call it not by the brand name, Taser, but by what it was—a conducted energy weapon, or "CEW." The problem was that CEW contains no hard consonants. It just slides out of the mouth like vanilla pudding. The word "Taser" sticks in the ear, has two consonants instead of three, and was just more fun to say. It was a battle we would never win, and soon enough, the term CEW was used only in the policy manual.

So, what does this mean for us as presenters? When you want to be funny, choose the right word. Often, the right word is the *more specific* one. "Macaque" is more specific and funnier than "monkey."

Here's an example from comedian Harrison Greenbaum. His bit is about what to do when your dog dies, you live in a studio apartment in New York, and you have to take it to a vet 20 blocks away. "So, what do you want me to do, just put, like, a dead dog in a backpack and go on the subway for four stops?! There's a sign, 'If you see something, say something.' Dead dog in a backpack! Definitely a something. You see a paw sticking out of a JanSport you call somebody."[53] Notice how using the brand name of the backpack is funnier because it draws a particular image in your mind.

Put Your Punch Word at the End of the Joke

Consider these two sentences: "He tripped in the street and got hit by an Isuzu!" vs. "He got hit by an Isuzu when he tripped in the street!" The funny word is "Isuzu." It's funnier than just "a car," and by putting it at the end, it has the greatest impact.

Another great example of this was pointed out by comedian and author David Nihill.[54] In Barack Obama's 2011 address to Congress, he was trying to explain the complexities of government and how many departments might be involved in seemingly simple matters. He said, "The Interior Department is in charge of salmon while they're in fresh water, but the Commerce Department handles them when they're in salt water. I hear it gets even more complicated once they're smoked."[55] Notice how the punch word "smoked" comes at the end. He could have said, "I hear when they're smoked, it gets even more complicated." This is better than nothing, but you can see how a hard consonant punch word at the end of the joke creates a proper cue for the audience to laugh. Is this a gut buster? No, but it does get a few chuckles and smiles, which is a win.

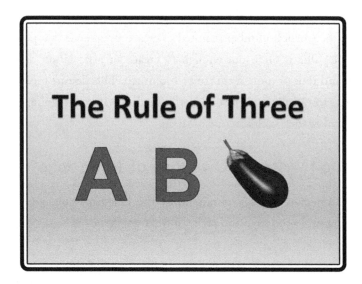

The Rule of Three

A bishop, a priest, and a rabbi walk into a bar. The genie will grant you three wishes. A redhead, a brunette, and a blond ... Why do soooo many jokes start like this? It's a time-tested formula, and here's how it works:

Set up, set up, punchline. Walk them down the garden path, and then turn on the sprinkler.

Here's an example from Jon Stewart, as told by David Nihill: "I celebrated Thanksgiving in an old-fashioned way. I invited everyone in my neighborhood to my house, we had an enormous feast, and then I killed them and took their land."[56]

And this from Laura Kightlinger: "I can't think of anything worse after a night of drinking than waking up next to someone and not being able to remember their name, or how you met, or why they're dead."

The setup creates an expectation that a third thing in your list will follow the first two. The third doesn't match and instead creates a sudden twist. This makes the final incongruent part unexpected and contradictory. It can't just be different—it has to relate to the first two.

Three is the smallest number required to create a sequence that people can anticipate. One is often not enough to create an expectation or enough tension and four or more seems to be too much. This doesn't mean it can't be done successfully—it's just harder to pull off. If you're going to write this as a joke, stick with the rule of three.

How Do I Write My Own Rule of Three Joke?

First, realize that nothing sounds funny the first time you write it. Get everything on to the page and *then* see what happens.

Here's an example. Let's say I want to make a joke about the Calgary Stampede. This is the world's largest outdoor show and is held for 10 days every summer. Think of a huge county fair in the middle of a city. There's a rodeo, midway, concerts, etc. It's an excuse for the whole city to dress Western and start day drinking.

Make a list of words that come to mind about the Stampede: cowboy hats, rodeo, Daisy Dukes, mini donuts, cotton candy, draft beer, BBQ, horses, crowds, deep-fried, fireworks, drunk, country music, bumper cars, expensive, chuck wagons, pancake breakfast, bulls, face painting, sunburn, regret.

The key is to get it all out without any judgment—don't worry about the funny. This is sometimes called the *peanut butter rule* … if you're making your list and you think of the word peanut butter, write it down.

Create a statement. Using the word "love" or "hate" can make this easier.

"I love the Stampede because …"

Next, we can answer our statement using the rule of three. The first two aren't meant to be funny. This is where we're setting up the joke.

I love the Stampede because

1. You're out in the sun,
2. You can ride bumper cars, and
3. You become nose-blind to the smell of draft beer and puke.

Is anyone going to pee their pants over this? No, but once again it creates the opportunity for a smile or a chuckle. The more you do this, the better you'll get at it. Test it out and adjust. As comic and public speaking world champion Darren LaCroix says, "Great jokes aren't written, they are rewritten."[57]

Funny Pictures

Adding funny pictures to your slide deck is a quick and easy way to make your presentation more fun and engaging. The trick here is to be a bit creative when looking for the funny.

Let's say that one of your takeaway messages is about spotting the danger in a situation. A Google image search for the word "danger" will bring up a bunch of signs that you'd expect to see (figure 1). Instead, try entering the search term "danger + funny." This will bring up a bunch of funny signs and pictures to do with danger (figure 2). This is funnier than the first sign, and many presenters stop there, but let's keep going.

Figure 1   *Figure 2*

> ## "When I was young, I was poor. But after decades of hard work, I am no longer young."
> —Bob Golen[58]

The key to comedy is surprise. This is why a joke is never as funny the second time you hear it. We need to give the audience something they don't expect, so now let's search for some synonyms for danger, like dangerous, hazard, risk, or threat. Remember that our message is about spotting the danger, so try this as well.

The great part about searching for images is that there are so many available, and clicking on one image will send you down a rabbit hole of even more related images. This type of search should get you off the obvious joke just enough to find a kickass image that will surprise your audience and get the point across.

Your biggest laugh will come when you *use the picture as the punchline*. This means knowing what slide is coming up next and setting up the laugh by saying something like, "We need to be better at spotting the danger signs." Then, use your presentation remote to advance to your punchline slide (figure 3). This image shows people doing dangerous stuff that they should know better about. The audience will create an image in their own mind about what may happen to them next.

Figure 3

Notice how these pictures don't have any text. They're funny immediately. Just because you found an amusing *New Yorker*–style comic strip that relates doesn't mean it's going to land. What takes away from a funny image is when the audience is required to read a sentence. This will mean that, depending on their reading speed, people will get the joke at different times. It's not terrible, but there's less of a shared funny moment.

Author Jeffrey Gitomer says, "At the end of laughter is the height of listening."[59] The best place for a funny image or joke is just before an important message. Using images is a fun and easy technique—now use it with purpose to get some smiles in your next presentation.

The End Justifies the Memes

By now I feel like everyone should know what a meme (pronounced meem) is. Think of it as an image, usually with some text that was added by a third party, that spreads quickly through social media. There are a ton of very funny ones out there, and they are a quick way to inject some smiles.

If you can't find one you like, *you can make your own* kickass meme. There are lots of websites and apps that allow you to do this—or you can do it right in PowerPoint. For the classic meme look, insert the image you want, then add text that is capitalized, in Impact font, colored white with a black outline. Done!

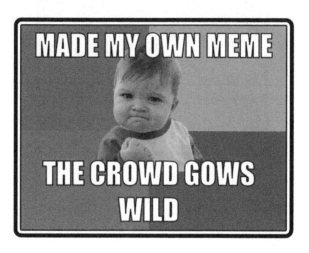

The Act Out

When telling a story where you mention another person, or even a particular object, it's funnier if you act as if you *are* them, instead of just talking *about* them. This is a performance for an audience after all! Think of any person, animal, or object and what their inner monologue might be in that situation. Become the characters.

Here's a quick example: I often bring candies or Halloween-sized chocolate bars with me when I teach to hand out as rewards for answering questions. I tell my classes that when I teach cops, they go, "I don't need any stupid chocolate bars." But then by the first break they're going, "Uh … can I have one of those bars?" This always gets a chuckle, and that's as simple as an act out needs to be. It's much funnier than saying, "Some of you may not want any chocolate now, but even cops want one by the first break."

This can even be done with objects. For example, "I shouldn't have eaten so much cheesecake because it's bad for my heart," vs., "As I dug into my second piece of cheesecake, my heart was like, 'Danny, you're killing me here!' "

The second one is clearly funnier. You don't even have to do a special voice or make any huge gestures, just act out what your heart was saying.

One technique for adding some punch to an act out is to physically move into a difference space when acting as that person. All this requires is stepping to one side while saying what one person said. This works especially well when recounting an interaction between you and someone else. Just imagine a taped square on the floor. Step into the square when acting as one person and out of it for another.

Another way to use this technique is to act out what someone or something is thinking or saying in an image.

"Hello? What do I gotta do to get some service around here?"

If you've got a funny friend or coworker, pay attention to how they tell stories. Stories are usually funnier when the teller acts out what people are saying. Listen for the words, "And I was like …," or "And this guy was like …" Chances are what follows is an act out.

To see some act out masters at work, check out any comedy by Brian Regan, Jim Gaffigan, or Bill Burr.

Tags

Tag lines are extra punchlines added to your existing joke. You get more bang for your buck because the premise of the joke has already been established.

Here's an example in a joke from Amy Schumer:

> "I finally slept with my high school crush. But now he expects me to go to his graduation. Like I know where I'm going to be in three years!"[60]

The first line is the setup and the second is the punchline. The third line is the tag that Amy said she discovered and added to this joke after performing it for years. Good tags are rarely obvious, and sometimes it takes someone else to spot a good tag for you.

I get that this is a more advanced technique, but if you've got a funny line that you like to use, see if you can add a tag to it. Look to write at least one tag line for each punchline. They might not all be winners, but some will be, and it's a good exercise to do. Tag lines are generally limited to two per punchline. Some comedians can pull off three or more, but it can start to get annoying and sound tired.

The Call Back

A call back simply *refers to an earlier joke or story*, often repeating the punchline in a new context. This creates a sense of connection and rapport between you and the audience because it now feels like you've got an inside joke that others wouldn't get because they weren't there for the first one.

This is where finding out a bit about the people in your audience can pay off. It's also worth your while to pay attention to the speakers who come before you so that you can tie in their material and call back to their jokes.

Here's an example: While working in a police academy with a brand-new class of officers, the instructors took turns introducing themselves, which included sharing one interesting thing about them. One instructor talked about how before becoming a cop he spent a university semester in Barbados breeding dolphins. Apparently, the dolphins needed help, and this involved getting into the water with them! This got a few chuckles, and the introductions moved on. The last instructor to introduce himself talked about his background and career, and then said with a straight face that the interesting thing about him was that he used to fly down to Barbados and dress up as a dolphin. The class erupted in laughter. It was a perfectly executed call back.

Tell a Joke

This topic is a minefield! Most speaking coaches will counsel against telling jokes, but since this is my book, you get my opinion. Joke telling can be difficult and nuanced. It's easier to give the blanket advice of "Don't do it." But I've seen it well executed many times, and I've done it successfully myself. It's ok to tell clean jokes so long as

- it relates to your topic and reinforces your point,
- it's funny, and
- you can tell it *well*.

One of my favorite speakers is Lt. Col. (Ret.) Dave Grossman, whom I've had the privilege of seeing speak on many occasions. He often uses jokes to hammer home a point.

One of his classics I heard him tell live goes like this: A soldier is about to go on leave and sees a sign on the base that says "Ocean Cruise $5—report to room 222." He thinks this is a great deal, so he goes up to room 222 with his cash in hand. When he walks in, he's quickly whacked on the head with a baseball bat. He wakes up bobbing in the ocean, tied to a log. His head hurts, and he feels like an idiot. As he's trying to figure out what happened, he sees a Marine who's also bobbing along, tied to another log. Not wanting to look foolish, he says to the Marine, "Do they serve any food on this here ocean cruise?"

To which the Marine replies, "Well, they didn't last year."

This joke always gets a laugh. The important part is that it speaks to the points he's making—that if something looks cheap and easy, maybe there's a catch and that just because we've always done something doesn't mean we should keep doing it.

When you hear a good joke, write it down or capture it somewhere. You may not even have a spot for it yet, but it may serve you well down the road. In the meantime, unless you're seasoned at it, practice telling it to real people (your family, friends, at parties, and at work) so that you can be smooth and confident in your delivery.

Use a Funny Quote

You don't have to write your own stuff! By using a quote from a comedian (or someone funny), you know it'll work. It's already been tested. Just give credit where it's due by saying, "As _____ once said ..."

As Will Ferrell once said, "Before you marry a person, you should first make them use a computer with slow internet to see who they really are."[61]

This will get a smile, and if it doesn't, that's ok. The attention isn't on you. This isn't your joke.

Here are a couple of quick examples:

> As George Carlin once said, "Singing is basically a form of pleasant, controlled screaming."[62]

> As Emily Blunt said in *The Devil Wears Prada*, "I'm one stomach flu away from my goal weight."[63]

Say the quote out loud as opposed to having the audience read it on a slide. That way everyone hears it at the same time and has that shared experience. They know it's supposed to be funny and will all laugh at the same time.

Putting It All Together

Let's use what we've learned to deconstruct a monologue by Ellen DeGeneres, taken from *The Ellen DeGeneres Show* in 2016:[64]

> Welcome to the show. I am Ellen and like many of you I am a baby-boomer. We are the generation that grew up drinking from garden hoses and drinking orange Tang and drinking from our parents' liquor cabinet (rule of three). Baby-boomers were born between 1946 and 1964. They call us that because after World War II there was a boom of babies being born. People were like, 'We lived through war, let's make whoopee' (act out). For you millennials making whoopee is like Netflix and chill—pause for huge laugh—but they were married (tag)—pause for even bigger laugh. Millennials were born between 1982 and 2004. These are people who will never know the joy of using the end of a pencil to dial the phone. Do you remember that? Where you would actually (she mimes dialing a rotary phone with a pencil—act out).

"In the land of the blind, the one-eyed man is king."
—Desiderius Erasmus[65]

Since most presenters don't intentionally try to use humor, it's not that hard to shine. It is absolutely worth your time to write some humorous stuff for your presentation. It doesn't always come easy, though—you have to work at it. Comedian and author Marshall Chiles says that writing humor is like going to the gym, which is why these are called exercises.[66] And you're competing against people who don't even work out.

Chapter Takeaways

1. The better you know your audience members, the better able you'll be to connect with them and call back to their experiences.
2. Punch up your stories with funny words.
3. Write a rule of three joke.
4. Include funny pictures and memes.
5. Act out what people or objects are thinking.
6. Collect jokes and learn to tell them well.
7. Use a funny quote.

Exercise

Write a rule of three joke. Start by picking something you either love or hate. Make a list of words or phrases associated with it. Remember that it doesn't need to be funny right out of the gate. You're just working a new muscle that will grow over time.

Chapter 6

DELIVER THE GOODS

You've done it! You've mastered your subject matter and built a kickass presentation that meets your objectives. Now it's time to think about other ways to add some awesome sauce: open with power; use confident body language; break the ice; and handle questions with panache.

Set the Stage

Get there early to get the room set up the way you want it. Here's a room checklist:

1. *Test your presentation equipment*—screen, projector, sound, video, and presentation remote. This always takes more time than you think it will.

2. *Teaching aids*—get the flip chart where you want it, have (working) whiteboard markers in the right spot, and set up any props where you need them.

3. *Lighting*—most importantly, can the audience see you from any point in the room? You are the presentation, not what's on the screen. Next, can they clearly see your screen from everywhere, especially at the back? Does the audience have enough light to be able to take notes?

4. *Seating*—this might be something you can't change, such as in an auditorium. If you've got a small class, you might want to move

the desks, chairs, and tables into a configuration you like. Maybe you'll use a hollow square where you can easily interact with each audience member or perhaps table groups that will be better for small group work.

5. *Remove clutter and distractions*—that flip chart with stuff from another class, the piles of paper and extra pens, even your own laptop bag and props. Tuck it all away so that the audience can focus on you.

6. *Check yourself*—before you wreck yourself! (Sorry, I couldn't resist.) Is your phone where you want it, and is it on silent?

*You'll find all the checklists again at the end of the book.

Now that you're set up you can focus on welcoming the audience members as they come in.

Calm Those Pre-Talk Nerves!

I'd been a speaker for years before I ever took to the stage as a stand-up comedian. I had somehow let a show producer talk me into entering a comedy talent show as my first time on stage! It felt like everything was working against me—my jokes were ready but completely untested, the audience was filled with my expectant friends and family, I was late to the venue, the set time was dropped from eight minutes down to seven, and I was freaking out about losing my place or just completely blanking!

The preshow meeting was just me, a cop, standing among a bunch of seasoned amateur comics. I felt like a fraud and kept thinking, "I don't think I belong here." As my stage time drew closer my fight-or-flight system kicked in, like my very life depended on this performance. My heart beat faster, my hands were sweating, and my mouth was dry. So, I did the only two things I could.

First and most importantly, I breathed. *Conscious, slow breathing lowers your heart rate.* In through the nose for a count of four, hold for four, out through the mouth for four, hold for four. Do it three times. This is often called combat breathing. It slows the sympathetic nervous system and reduces the flood of stress chemicals into your bloodstream. You can even teach this to kids by getting them to imagine smelling a flower, then blowing out a candle.

Second, I went to the bathroom and … stood in front of the mirror as if I were Superman. (I'm not much of a puker.) I recalled a great TED talk by Amy Cuddy on power posing.[67] *Standing like a boss might just trick your mind* into thinking that you're powerful. Putting your hands on your hips, arms behind your head, or stretching your arms out like a *Y* takes up space and shows that you're confident and in control (or at least comfortable in your surroundings).

I was still nervous, excited, and energized as I hopped up on stage, but at least I wasn't fumbling my words or having a complete brain stall. Though most of it was a blur, I got a few laughs. That show would turn out to be the first of many.

A little nervousness and excitement are good! It reminds you that you're alive and about to do something important. Know that everyone, including professional speakers, still get these feelings. If you've prepared properly, it should feel a bit like walking into an exam that you've studied for. Through mastering your content, rehearsing, and practicing breathing techniques, you won't get rid of the butterflies in your stomach, but you just might get them to fly in formation.

Rock Your Opening

> **"You've got seconds to grab your audience's attention and only minutes to keep it."**
>
> —John Medina, author of *Brain Rules*.[68]

A kickass opening will

1. engage the audience's attention,
2. establish a connection with the audience, and
3. introduce the premise or main idea of your presentation.

The audience will make up their minds if they like you or not in the first 30 seconds. One of the easiest things you can do to get them on your side is to *smile*. When you smile you convey warmth and confidence. This needs to be a genuine or Duchenne smile. That means smiling with your eyes, not just your mouth. Humans are remarkably perceptive, and our subconscious minds pick up and make inferences on these small expressions. Opening with some humor or a story lets the audience see a bit of your personality and can set the tone for the entire presentation.

If you're teaching a class or presenting in a work setting, chances are you'll be introducing yourself, so it'll be up to you to get things going. Even with adults, you can't trust that everyone will be paying attention to the clock and suddenly quiet down so that you can start speaking—or can you?

Imagine that you're at the front of a crowded classroom where everyone is chatting or looking at their phones. The obvious way to get everyone's attention is to get loud so that the audience can hear you over the din. "OK everyone! Let's get started!" Sound familiar? A more effective method is to

1. stand in the power position of the room. This means to the left of the screen as the audience sees it. People read left to right, and their eyes will go to you first.
2. stand still with your arms at your sides and be quiet.

That's it.

But wait, aren't we trying to command attention? Of course … and here's what will happen. A few people will stop what they're doing and will wait for you to begin. Others will catch on until the room is quiet and all eyes and ears are on you. Attention grabbed with no yelling involved.

Memorize your opening line. This ensures that you're being *purposeful* about what you'll say. I can hear the excuses now: "That's fine, but I don't want to sound rehearsed." Have you ever watched a TED talk and thought, "This speaker's opening sounds too rehearsed?" I doubt it. TED Talks are some of the most rehearsed presentations out there, and they're so good because people spend the time to get it right.

What not *to say*—You've got their attention; now don't screw it up by saying something predictable and cliché, like: "Good evening, ladies and gentlemen. What I'm going to talk to you about today is …" This is not engaging.

Don't say, "I'm sooo excited to be here!" And especially don't say, "Good morning!" [wait for response] "Well, that wasn't very energetic. I said, 'Good morning!' " Guh … shoot me now.

Don't introduce your subject as being boring. "Hey everyone, I know this topic is dry, but we've got to get through it." How does that help? This is your presentation—if it's dry, it's because you're making it dry.

Don't tell the audience that you're new to the topic. Aren't you supposed to know more about this than anyone in the room?

Don't tell the audience that you're nervous! All you're doing is trying to lower their expectations so that they can tell you afterward, "You did great!" even if you sucked.

Your first words matter. They should be the *hook* that grabs the audience immediately. Here are some ways to engage the audience with something memorable right from the start.

Say something provocative. An unusual statistic or a counterintuitive fact that relates to your message. For example, "There are more trees on earth than stars in the Milky Way." [69] Or, "If you want someone to like you, get them to do you a favor, not the other way around." [70]

Share a quote. Allen Saunders said, "Life is what happens when you're busy making other plans." Or Albert Einstein said, "Imagination is more important than knowledge."[71]

Ask a question that gets the audience thinking. Ask for a show of hands—this gets them involved right away. For example, "How many of you wish you had more hours in a day?" Or how about asking a true-or-false question?

"Imagine ..." By starting with this word, you can lead your audience through a sensory experience right off the top. For example, "Imagine this. You're a parent to a toddler, and you wake early in the morning. The complete silence coming from your child's room gives you a feeling that something is off. You step into the hallway and notice a slight cool breeze on your skin and the smell of fresh rain. That's not right. You check your child's bed—empty. Where is she? You sprint down the stairs to see that your front door is wide open. This can't be happening!" Already they're fully engaged and wanting to know—needing to know—what happens next.

Tell a story. Opening with a story, especially a well-constructed one, will grab your audience's attention. There's no need to say, "I'm going to tell you a story about ..." All eyes are on you, so you can launch right in. "It was a brisk morning in January 1976 ..."

One option with this is to stop the story at a point before the ending. This leaves the audience in suspense, allowing you to finish the story in your closing as a bookend to the presentation. See more about stories in the section on storytelling in chapter 4.

Use a prop. Do you own a unique item, a tool, or an antique? Tell a story about it, or use it as an analogy. As long as it ties in with your message, it will grab your audience's attention.

Once you've made your opening, you'll need to *build a bridge to your message*. How does it relate to what you're talking about? Why is this quote important? What does this story illustrate?

Your Introduction

> "Allow myself to introduce ... myself."
>
> —Austin Powers[72]

After your opening you can move into letting the audience know who you are. Write and practice your intro so that you don't pull an Austin Powers.

Don't be so arrogant to assume that everyone knows who you are and what you're all about. The same goes for work presentations where you might assume everyone already knows you. I've lost track of how many times I've been in a class where the instructor just launches into their material without so much as saying their name. This leaves people in the audience asking their neighbors, "Who the heck is this?"

If you don't give your audience enough of your background, they may be left wondering why they should listen to you. I once attended a course where the instructor said as his opening, "I'm not going to tell you who I am or what I've done. Now, let's begin." Um, what?! This was how he chose to start off a weeklong course of training police instructors? In this environment credibility was king, and this guy was starting off with none.

Stick with *relevant* credentials. If your presentation is about physics, then the audience likely doesn't need to hear that you've also run 100 marathons. Some speakers try way too hard to establish themselves as the obvious expert in their topic by listing every certificate, course, award, and accolade they've ever earned. Not only can this eat up valuable time, but it can also cause you to come across as pompous.

Aim to give the Goldilocks of introductions—not too long and not too short. What does that mean? A couple of sentences. Be honest and be humble. Then, run it by some people you trust who will give you feedback. My preference is to give the audience enough at the start that they want to listen, and then inevitably, I'll end up revealing other bits of my experience along the way. Ultimately, if you do a great job of delivering the presentation, your credibility will shine through.

Next, let them know what you're going to be speaking about and *why it matters to them*. Tune them into the radio station *WIIFM—what's in it for me*? What will the audience gain from this? What problem will you solve? How will this make their life easier?

What If Someone Is Introducing You?

If you're speaking at a conference or event, you may have someone introducing you. Always *supply them with an intro* that they can read word for word. An intro is not a bio. Do not send them your résumé and hope that it goes well, because it likely won't. A great guideline for your supplied introduction is that it contains three short paragraphs:

1. Who you are and what you do
2. What establishes your credibility on the subject
3. How your presentation relates to the audience—what's in it for them?

Make sure the last sentence ends with your name. Just like a punchline, this lets the audience know that the introduction is over and that they can start clapping. For example, "Ladies and gentlemen would you please welcome Dr. Jimmy Bloggins." Do not speak during the applause! Wait for the applause to end, pause for moment, then start with your engaging opening.

Let's recap the steps to a great opening:

1. The hook—grab them with a question, statement, or story.
2. The bridge—how does the hook relate to your message?
3. The intro—share a couple of sentences about you relative to your presentation.
4. WIIFM—what's in it for me? What problem of theirs are you solving?

How to Build Trust and Credibility

As speaking coach Mark Brown puts it: *Authenticity + Vulnerability = Credibility.* Trust and credibility are critical because you need the audience to believe what you're saying. They don't expect perfection, but they do expect honesty and integrity. If the audience already knows and likes you, then you're ahead of the game. Regardless of whether they know you or not, the same behaviors will help you to earn their trust and position you in their minds as a person of credibility.

1. *Use personal stories.* A little self-disclosure through stories lets the audience into your world and into your thought process. Use examples of how you've used the material you're presenting—and it's ok if it's an example of something you did badly. If you can show how you messed up but learned a lesson, you come across as relatable and human.

2. *Give them an experience.* My wife and I once had a part-time private practice doing hypnotherapy, and one of my wife's specialties was hypnosis for childbirth. She would run classes for parents-to-be in our living room, teaching the husbands what to say and do during the birth to keep everything calm and comfortable. An important lesson was the power of the mind to block out pain. Women's bodies are designed for childbirth, but it's hard for a soon-to-be mother to imagine anything but the screaming torture she's seen so many times on TV.

One exercise my wife would do with both partners was to put an ice cube on their forearm and hold it there with a piece of plastic wrap. This became painful fairly quickly. The couples then learned that they could turn that discomfort up and down like a dial—all with their minds. I've done this same exercise myself a few times, and that experience gave me the confidence that it really works. The experience was sticky because it was tangible and surprising.

3. *Admit when you're wrong.* Nobody's perfect. The ability to change your mind or your perspective is disarming. The same goes for admitting that you don't know something. Just because you're presenting doesn't mean that you've magically got all the answers.

4. *Take responsibility.* Someone else was supposed to bring a prop for you and forgot? So what? A professional will improvise without mentioning it and move on. Blaming the venue for the lack of heat or the city for the construction that "caused" you to be late only looks bad on you. It's your presentation, so take ownership.

5. *Know your sources.* Where, exactly, did this info come from? We often hear people saying they read a "recent study." Chances are they didn't read the actual study but a summary of it somewhere else. That's typical, and it's ok. If you want to cite a research study, it's a good idea to know some details about it—who, what, when, where, why, and how—which will be more credible than just giving your audience a finding. This extra work is all part of mastering your subject.

6. *Give credit.* Chances are that not everything in your presentation was your idea. You don't have to cite every source, but don't pass off material as yours when it's not.

7. *Tell the truth.* This seems obvious, but we've all been in presentations where our BS meter is jumping. There's no quicker way to lose credibility and trust than to get caught in an exaggeration or a lie.

8. *Like likes like.* We like people who are like us. As a presenter, you will have opportunities to empathize with your audience and to show that you know what it's like to be in their shoes. For example, "I remember when I heard this for the first time and, like you, I thought there was no way it could be true." Introductions and ice-breakers give you a chance to have some "me too" moments (the good kind!) with individual audience members. It's one of the oldest sales techniques in the book: Find something you have in common with the customer, and they're more likely to buy what you're selling.

9. *Start on time,* come back from breaks on time, and finish on time. When you don't hold up your end of the bargain, how can you expect the audience to do the same for you?

10. *Embody your message.* You've got to walk the walk. How you present yourself and everything about your character, knowledge, experience, and values must be in alignment with what you're saying. You can't speak with authority on fitness when you're 50 pounds overweight and sipping a can of Coke. You can't roll out ethics training to your company when half of them know that you got caught bumping uglies in the file room last year with that cutie in accounting.

Kickass Housekeeping

This is another contentious activity that I've seen done well, and I've also seen it done where the presenter makes a room full of adults feel as if they're back in kindergarten.

You may be the first speaker of the day in a facility that's unfamiliar to the audience. If so, you'll want to quickly cover a few things like emergency exits, the location of the washrooms and cafeteria, breaks (how frequent and how long), food and drinks in the room, notes, handouts, and tests.

Adults don't need to be told to silence their phone. I like to let them know that this is an adult learning environment and that if they need to step out to answer a call, then go right ahead. The idea is to *be so engaging* that they don't feel the urge to text or game under the table. You know you're losing them when all you can see is the top of people's heads as they stare at their glowing crotches!

Depending on the type of presentation you're giving, you may also want to address how the audience can ask questions. My recommendation is to *encourage questions at any time*, which will help generate discussion and increase engagement. The whole "save your questions until then end" thing shows a lack of confidence in the material and in your ability to present while interacting with the audience.

One technique I've seen to bring the group back from discussion is for the presenter to hold their hand in the air. Everyone in the room is supposed to stop talking and do the same until all is quiet. Now, one of the lessons I learned in the military was that if something is stupid and it works, it's not stupid. This is an exception! If you want a room of professionals to feel like dummies—and to think you're one—use this technique.

Do We Need Ground Rules?

I've been in several presentations where the instructor has a class discussion about the "rules" for the class. Everyone throws out ideas for proper classroom etiquette, like turn off your phone, don't interrupt whoever is speaking, respect everyone's ideas, be back from breaks on time, etc. The presenter writes them on a flip chart or whiteboard and the list of rules is there for all to see throughout. The idea is that if the audience generates the list themselves, they'll have more buy-in and are more likely to follow their own rules.

I can't think of a time when this was needed. Overall, people know how to behave, and this type of list causes the audience to feel like a shifty teen whose parents are going out for night.

Give Them a Break!

People need and appreciate breaks. As a presenter, it's very easy to get caught up in speaking to the point where you're not aware of your audience's mood or needs. I aim to give breaks at least every hour, and I make sure the audience knows that this is my plan.

Breaks don't have to be 15 minutes long each time. Some breaks need only be for five minutes—enough for people to stretch their legs, get urine out, get coffee in, and then get back to it. Some presenters use a slide with a countdown timer, but I haven't found this to be necessary. One trick I do use is to *give them an odd number of minutes* for their break. For some reason, knowing they have nine or 11 minutes causes people to pay more attention to their watches.

I was once in a presentation where the speaker didn't stop talking for three hours straight! This wasn't a fun and engaging presentation but more like the ramblings of a bitter old man. Since no one knew if or when there would be a break, people just started getting up on their own to step out to the bathroom. No one wanted to go back and eventually three-quarters of the audience was out in the hallway on their phones, with only a handful of poor souls trapped inside the room like hostages. The presenter didn't seem to notice, and if he did, he didn't care.

Ice-Breakers

Some students love a good get-to-know-you activity while others want to just melt into their seats and disappear. Most presentations won't require them, but some will benefit from students connecting with each other, which will increase their comfort level in participating.

You should use ice-breakers when you have lots of time—think half-day to multiday presentations, especially where participants will be interacting with each other. Some ice-breakers can take from 20 to 30 minutes, so make sure the juice is worth the squeeze.

Here are a few that I've seen done well:

1. *One Interesting Thing.* In this very basic ice-breaker, the presenter just goes around the room having audience members introduce themselves with basics, like where they're from, perhaps their experience with the subject matter, and one interesting thing about themselves. This might be a weird hobby, an experience they had, their last vacation, etc. It can sometimes take a bit of gentle prodding by the presenter as occasionally audience members will say something like, "There's nothing interesting about me," but it's a great way to learn about the audience so that you can refer back to people's experiences throughout your presentation.

2. *SNOHKAY.* This stands for something no one here knows about you. Give audience members a few minutes to use a marker and flip chart paper to prepare their introduction by drawing pictures. This can include where they're from, a favorite hobby, something about their family, etc. Then, go around the room and have each person introduce themselves using their drawings. The interesting part is the final thing, the SNOHKAY. This is great for learning about your audience and having fun and interesting things to tie into your presentation.

3. *Same-same.* Put people in groups of two to five. Have them come up with a few things they have in common. The key is for this to be specific, not, "We all have brown hair." Maybe they have the same favorite movie, play the same sport, listen to the same podcast, drive the same car, etc. Then have them share this with the larger group while at the same time introducing themselves. This works well because like likes like—we like people who are like us. This gets some creative juices flowing and goes a long way to establishing rapport, which will help during small-group work later on.

4. *Two Truths and a Lie.* Each person comes up with two truthful statements about themselves and one lie. The trick is to have the lie sound plausible enough to blend in. Then, go around the room

to have people introduce themselves, give their two truths and a lie, and have the rest try to guess which is the lie. This is a fun game that always gets a laugh.

Body Language

As a species, humans had nonverbal language for a long time before we developed the spoken word. This is why if your body language doesn't match the words you say, people will believe the body. Try it—turn to a friend and say, "I like your shirt," while rolling your eyes. Despite your words this won't be taken as a compliment.

Most presenters, especially starting out, are not aware of their body language. This seems far less important a thing to concentrate on than, for example, remembering what to say. Here's where we go back to the principle of mastering your content. It's only when you have an iron grip on your content that some space is freed up inside your mind to pay attention to what you're doing at the same time.

Turn on the camera! A great way to evaluate your body language is by watching yourself on video. I get it—most of us would rather lick a razor blade than watch ourselves present. (That's a bit visceral, I know.) But it's a great way to get immediate and undeniable feedback about what your body language is communicating.

In her memoir, *Becoming*, Michelle Obama talks of being shocked by stories depicting her as angry in the lead up to the 2008 election. Obama strategist and campaign chief David Axelrod had her watch the video of her speeches with the volume turned off to observe her body language. She said, "I saw my expression as a stranger might perceive it, especially if it was framed with an unflattering message. I could see how the opposition had managed to dice up these images and feed me to the public as some sort of pissed-off harpy."[73]

Smile. This is so simple and yet so overlooked. About half the people in the world are "people" people and the other half are "task" people. Just think about some of the people you know. Some always seem to be smiling. These people tend to gravitate toward jobs where people are involved, like sales or customer service.

Others rarely smile and tend toward jobs working with things or numbers, like engineers or accountants. Even when things are going great, it doesn't seem to show on their face. If you're one of those people, you need to understand that half of the people you meet are judging you on the fact that you don't smile. They are the "people" people and what they think is, "This person doesn't smile, so they must not be happy."

I'm not asking you to go around with a fake smile on all the time, but just be conscious of it. There are times in a presentation (like during your introduction and when answering questions) when smiling will go a long way toward building trust and rapport.

Lose the Podium

You are the presentation—so get out from behind that podium! In fact, if they'll let you, get rid of it all together. I want you to think about every presentation you've sat in where the speaker or speakers stood behind a podium. Do any of these stand out as being kickass? I doubt it.

People are there to see you, and they can't do that if you're gripping an oak box that covers 70% of your body. Thankfully, podiums are becoming less common every year, and even theaters with them will often provide a microphone that you can carry or wear so that you can be free to move and not be tethered like a raccoon in leghold trap.

What to Do with Your Hands

According to body language expert Blanca Cobb, hands are an emotional highlighter for what you're saying.[74] This means that *they enhance and draw attention to emotions you're conveying*, whether consciously or not. Have you ever watched a speaker who just keeps their arms at their sides? They end up looking like an alien being trying to communicate like a person.

We all gesture with our hands as we talk, even people who are blind from birth. Gestures are a fundamental part of communication, not just some add-on that helps us get our point across. Our brains love seeing hand gestures, and they are key to engaging the audience. Here are three basic types of hand gestures to get you going:

1. **Open palms**—this makes me think of nearly every sculpture of Jesus. When we show our palms to the audience, it communicates openness and honesty. This can be done with fingers up, down, or to the side.
2. **Baton gestures**—think of an orchestra conductor holding that small chopstick-looking thing between their thumb and index finger. The hand moves along with the rhythm of your speech. This can be done with just your index finger, two fingers, or even your whole hand. President Bill Clinton was famous for doing this with his thumb resting on top of his fist.
3. **Functional gesturing**—use your hands to help tell the story or reinforce a point. Here are just a few examples:

Are you pointing out three key steps? Then hold up fingers to go along with each step.

Are you talking about a timeline? Then use your hands in front of you to mark the start and then the end of the timeline—like you're showing how big the fish was that got away. (Remember that we read left to right. The audience is facing you, so they're opposite to you. This means starting a timeline gesture with your right hand and ending with your left.)

Touch your chest when talking about yourself. For example, try it when saying, "I don't see an issue with this."

Use each hand to indicate opposing ideas or issues. "On one hand it's cold as hell up there, and on the other they've got wicked skiing."

Overall, more gesturing is better, and we want to hit the midrange of gesturing—somewhere between constant jazz hands and Monty Burn's pensive tented fingers.

What to avoid? Anything that displays a closed posture: crossed arms, hands on hips, arms behind your back, hands clasped in front, hands in pockets, etc. Every time I think about this, I go back to my seventh grade teacher who constantly jingled his keys in his pocket as he talked.

Pointing. It's ok to point, for example, when saying, "Now this is important." We just want to avoid pointing *at* people because it comes across as accusatory and rude. When I was learning to be an instructor in the army, it was beaten into us never to point with a finger, but instead to use all the fingers together. The "knife hand" is widely known and correctly mocked by anyone who has served. If you do decide to keep your fingers together to gesture toward an audience member, simply rotate your hand a bit so that your palm is up. This shows openness instead of assertiveness.

Stand and Land

It's great to move around, so long as it's with purpose. However, when you get to a key point or a punchline, stand still! This means understanding what your key messages are and being purposeful about delivering them. It also means rehearsing these movements. Use a video of your rehearsal or another presentation to give you feedback about how you tend to move so that you can eliminate swaying and random pacing.

Engage Them with Eye Contact

Why does the advice to make eye contact seem to be a cliché? New presenters often struggle with this and are sometimes told to pick a spot on the wall at the back of the room and look at it or even to look at a spot between audience members. I guess this is better than staring at your shoes, but not by much. Audience members are there for the personal connection, so you need to speak to them, not at them.

Have you ever had a conversation with someone where they didn't make eye contact with you? They looked at the wall, your shirt, their coffee, or the floor. It's just weird. We feel odd and left out because there's no shared experience. It may leave you feeling like the person didn't like you or even trust you.

Body language expert Allan Pease describes it this way:

> "When person A likes person B, he will look at him a lot. This causes B to think that A likes him, so B will like A in return. In other words, in most creatures, to build a good rapport with another person, your gaze should meet theirs about 60% to 70% of the time. This will also cause them to begin to like you. It is not surprising, therefore, that the nervous, timid person who meets our gaze less than one-third of the time is rarely trusted." [75]

Trust isn't the only reason. *Eye contact speaks to confidence.* Most police academies require their fledgling officers to look people in the eye and acknowledge them. I've spent a lot of time in these environments, and it can even get a bit annoying when passing a line of recruits coming the other way because each one will say, "Good morning, sir," as they pass. But it's teaching them a valuable lesson in that how they carry themselves—and the confidence they project—matters.

Think of your presentation as a conversation with many people at once. The fact is that *there is no audience, but a group of individuals.* If you look at the back wall or between people, the individuals in the room never experience eye contact with you and won't get the corresponding hit of the bonding hormone, oxytocin. You are the presentation, and the audience is there for that personal connection. As a presenter, you should also be looking to connect with them.

Even in an auditorium, your goal should be to make eye contact with specific faces and speak to them as if you're in a conversation. In her book *Daring Greatly*, renowned author and speaker Dr. Brené Brown recounted an experience where she was super nervous before delivering a TED talk in Long Beach.

"When I finally walked onto the stage the first thing I did was make eye contact with several people in the audience. I asked the stage manager to bring up the houselights so I could see people. I needed to feel connected."[76]

That connection helped her to feel grounded. When I started doing comedy at clubs, I noticed that the stage lights are bright and close, and the audience is completely in the dark. All you can see are the people in the front row or two, and beyond them is a sea of blackness. You can't see faces—all you can do is listen for their laughter (or lack thereof!). I found this strange and unnerving because I wasn't getting that personal connection I was used to.

Round 'em up! Here's a great piece of advice from the late, great comedian Ralphie May: When you're getting to an important message (or punchline), use eye contact to round up the audience like sheep. [77] Look at an audience member on the left or right wing, and then do the same on the other side. Do this while what you're saying is leading up to your important message. This brings everyone's attention toward you as you deliver your punch to someone in the middle of the room.

Ask Better Questions

> **"Question marks are shaped like hooks and all I'm doing is hooking into your brain and drawing your attention back to me as the presenter."**
>
> —Mark Robinson[78]

Why is asking questions a good thing? (Notice that your mind is now looking for the answer. See what I did there?) Posing questions is a kickass way to gain and maintain engagement and keep your audience's attention.

There are a couple of ways to do this:

1. Turn normal sentences into questions. Here, we don't expect the audience to have the answer—we'll do that for them. For example, "The main reason why people decide to get a dog is for companionship," vs., "Why do most people decide to get a dog? Companionship."

Notice how even though you know the answer, your mind is searching for what it thinks it already knows. This keeps you engaged.

2. Ask a question that someone in the audience needs to answer.

If you ask a specific person for the answer before you pose the question, the rest of the audience feels like they're off the hook. "James, did they or did they not hold the Olympics during WWII?" Everyone can now tune out because they aren't in the hot seat.

A better way is to pose the question first, and then choose someone to answer it. This often results in the people who know the answer putting their hand up. The method I'm going to advocate works whether anyone puts their hand up or not. Some hard-core adopters of this technique consider this a "no hands up" questioning strategy, meaning that they tell the audience ahead of time not to raise their hands. The best way is to try it yourself and see what works.

The method is called *pose, pause, pounce, bounce.*

Pose—Ask the question to the audience.

Pause—Give students a chance to think. You have to be ok with the short silence while people think about their answer.

Pounce—Choose someone to answer. If you want this to be truly random in a classroom setting, there are several methods you can use to choose a student, such as rolls of dice (where each student has been assigned a number), choosing names from a hat, or random name generators.

Bounce—Before confirming the answer, ask someone else, either to challenge the answer or create some discussion. "James said yes. Sarah, do you agree? How come?"

Another method is to call on a person who you know knows the answer. Maybe this is because you already know them, or you've talked about this subject with them beforehand. "Christie, in your experience as a paramedic, how often would you say that you need to use restraints to keep patients on the stretcher?" This is especially good if you've got someone in your audience who is an expert or has loads of experience about what you're asking.

I Want Candy!

I use candy—Hi-Chews, mints, chocolates, caramels, Halloween-sized bars, etc.—as a reward for participation and not just for correct answers. This might seem childish in an adult learning environment, but hear me out. I've done this for years while training police officers. At first some will try to play tough and say, "I don't need any candy," but it's not long before they've got their hand up too.

This gets everyone paying attention and engaging in the material. It also gets me walking around the room to hand it out—or at least not throwing a Hail Mary pass from the front of the room. Should you try this during your next TEDx talk? No. Use your common sense—this isn't going to be appropriate in every presentation setting.

What Questions Do You Have?

I learned years ago, from mentor and presentation master Brian Willis, that asking, "What questions do you have?" gets better results than simply asking, "Any questions?" Asking, "What questions do you have?" assumes that the audience will have questions and makes it easy for them to ask. Sometimes, "Any questions?" or even, "Questions?" is interpreted as a something challenging and not welcoming. It's like ending with, "Clear as mud?" or, "Does that make sense?" When no one in the audience raises their hand, everything must be good, right?

The assumption by the presenter is that their information was so complete that no one would dare challenge their awesomeness. I see "Any questions?" more like a rhetorical question or simply one that makes it more difficult to respond to because there's a fear of standing out. Remember—it's not about you; it's about your audience.

When I was in basic training with the army, the instructors did not like being questioned and you didn't want to do anything to draw attention to yourself. The army was full of rhetorical questions. If the platoon was standing in formation and about to head out to some activity, an instructor might say something like, "Does everyone have their rain gear?" If you happened to be the poor sap who just now realized that you didn't have yours with you, it made it even tougher to speak up. You were better to keep your mouth shut and pray for sunny skies.

As an instructor and leader in the army, and later in the police, I learned to ask questions in a different way. It wasn't about intimidating people—it was about making sure the people in your charge were prepared. A better way to ask would be "Is there anyone here who *does not* have their rain gear?" I've used this slight change in questioning many times as a presenter.

When going into small groups, it's easy for people to sheepishly say nothing when you ask questions like, "Does everyone have a pencil? Good. Go ahead and begin." This is where anyone who doesn't have a pencil will be subtly asking the people around them or trying to find something that will suffice in its place. Replace that with "Before we start, is there anyone who does not have a pencil?" Do this while holding up a few spares to hand out, and those who weren't prepared now have they what they need without losing face.

If you let the audience know that they can ask questions at any time, there shouldn't be a bunch at the end. If no questions arise, you can ask, "What questions do you have?" at the end of segments or before breaks. This means that you don't need a "Questions?" slide at the end of your deck, and you can go right into a review or close.

Handling Questions from the Audience

Even if you've done your best to prepare for tough questions during your presentation, they're going to come up. It's not just about the answer itself—you must also give thought to, and practice, how you'll deliver your answer.

The best breakdown of question handling that I've ever seen comes from Mark Horstman at Manager Tools. I've used this technique (yes, it's a technique) for years with great results. It's called *catching the medicine ball.*[79] When faced with a question from the audience, follow these steps:

1. Make eye contact and smile—this shows confidence and openness (especially when the question is a direct challenge toward you).
2. Take a step toward the questioner—this acknowledges them and shows that you're confident enough to share the floor (the power) with them. If you have the space, you can get even closer to them.
3. Say yes and use their name.
4. Raise your eyebrows—this powerful facial expression sends the signal that you're open. Think about what you do with your eyebrows when saying hello to a baby. Your eyebrows exist to protect your eyes, and raising them shows that you're lowering your defenses and allows the other person to see your eyes better.
5. Lean slightly forward—this happens at whatever point you stop at in moving toward your questioner. Keep one foot ahead of the other, as if you're leaning in to shake someone's hand. Because you'll be standing and they are likely sitting, this lowers your body a small amount and reduces your height relative to them.

6. Keep your hands down with your fingers pointing mainly downward and your palms facing mainly toward the questioner—as if you were going to catch a medicine ball being tossed at you between your waist and knees. This prevents you from crossing your arms or displaying some other closed posture.

7. Throughout the question keep smiling, keep nodding, and keep eye contact.

8. When they finish their question, you "catch the medicine ball." Lean back a little, rock back slightly onto your back foot, and move your hands up toward your chest with your palms facing more toward you (or even clasping them). This lets you take back the floor (and control) from the questioner.

9. You may have to repeat the question (if the group is large enough to require it) to ensure that everyone hears it. This means that you're now speaking to the whole audience and not just to the questioner.

10. When you start to answer the question, look at the questioner only during the first part of your answer. This lets them know that you're answering their question but that you're also speaking to a larger group of people and that they deserve an answer as well. Moving your eye contact back to the audience prevents you from getting into a dialogue with the questioner, which is important, especially if they are a detractor.

11. Conclude your answer with eye contact with the questioner. This shows them and the rest of the audience that you have confidence in your answer (especially if you feel you're being challenged).

12. Ask the questioner, "Have I answered your question?" This is especially helpful early on in your presentation because it sets the tone that you can confidently handle tough questions (especially if you've nailed your answer). This alone may prevent questions from detractors later. You do not need to do this for every question, especially if things are going well and the questions you get are not a challenge to your material.

Wow, I know this seems like a lot of steps, but some of them happen concurrently (like steps 1–4). Is it a lot to remember? Of course! This goes back to the principle of *mastering your content*. When we know our stuff, it frees up space in our minds to focus on our own body language as well as the body language of our audience.

What about the *serial questioner*? You know, the person who just has to ask a ton of questions to challenge you and try to take some of your power away.

Serial questioners are to presenters what hecklers are to comedians—if it hasn't happed yet, it's only a matter of time. You can prepare as much as you like, but sometimes you just gotta deal with it when it comes. The rest of the audience usually doesn't like this person, and they want to see you do well. If you've done your job building trust with the audience by being both professional and humble, you'll find that they may even come to your aid.

With a serial questioner, don't end your answer with eye contact with them, and certainly don't ask them, "Have I answered your question?"

You can take it a step further by turning your back to them and carrying on with your material immediately after answering. This means that they don't have eye contact with you and now have to get your attention to ask their next question. You can say, "Now back to …" Avoid saying, "Where were we?" as you come back to your presentation. It just hands your detractor a win because everyone now knows you've been thrown off.

Be as *direct and specific* in your answer as possible. For example, if they ask a yes/no question, start with that. "Yes, and the reason is …" or even, "It depends on two factors …" What we want to avoid is waffling political answers that don't actually answer the question.

It's ok to say, "I don't know." Some questions just don't have an answer. If it's something you can find out, let that person know that you'll follow up at a later date with the answer—and then be sure to follow up.

Closing

You've wowed your audience by providing entertainment and value. You've reviewed what you covered and maybe even had some sort of quiz. You've handled their questions and thanked them for their attention, and now it's time to bring this thing in for a landing. Just like your opening, *a kickass close needs to be done with purpose.*

A weak close can take the air out of an otherwise great presentation. Whereas your opening sets up the premise or main idea, the close should reinforce it. Go back to your mission: What do you want your audience to think, feel, know, or do? If you have a call to action, what's their next step?

Don't Leave Them Hanging

Have you ever left a presentation as an audience member with lingering questions? "So, what ended up happening to that lady?" Or, "Did they go on to win the air band contest or not?" This is more common in formal presentations where the audience doesn't ask questions. As a presenter, you likely won't even realize that you left your audience wondering about a few details. This is where feedback in rehearsal is key so that you can identify and close any open loops.

Especially relevant for more formal presentations is to *avoid the double close.* This is when you wrap it up with "In conclusion ..." or "I'll leave you with this ...," and then you continue to talk or take questions. Not powerful.

Speaker Mark Brown relates a close that occurred during the murder trial of former NFL star and actor OJ Simpson in the mid-1990s. During the prosecutor's passionate address to the jury, he gave the line, "Ron Goldman was in the wrong place at the wrong time. Nicole Brown Simpson was in the wrong place for a long time." [80] Boom! A powerhouse close ... that never happened. Sadly, the prosecutor kept talking and missed the opportunity for a perfect closing line. Remember that *your final words linger.*

Consider ending with a quote or a short story that reinforces your message and leaves an impression.

Chapter Takeaways

1. Set your stage by working through a checklist.
2. Build a strong opening and have it memorized.
3. Build trust and credibility by being authentic.
4. Some ice-breaker activities will go a long way to increasing participation and engagement.
5. Be purposeful with your body language, especially hand gestures and eye contact.
6. Ask better questions using the pose, pause, pounce, bounce method.
7. Handle questions by catching the medicine ball.
8. Close your presentation with purpose.

Exercises

Learn to use breathing to bring down your heart rate. Try it right now—you can keep your eyes open. Breathe in through your nose for a count of four, hold for four, breathe out through the mouth for four, hold for four. Do this three times and notice how much more relaxed you feel. Use this technique often, and it'll be there when you need it. In fact, try it the next time someone is taking your pulse or blood pressure—they'll tell you to stop it!

Capture a portion of your next presentation or rehearsal on video. Watch 30 seconds of it, and pay close attention to your body language—your facial expressions, posture, and hands gestures. What did you do well? What will you change in the future?

Take a critical look at one current presentation you deliver, and write a purposeful opening. Start by brainstorming a list of quotes, questions, props, or engaging stories that might work and then rehearse them out loud. Refine your choice and make it part of your next presentation.

Chapter 7

SPECIAL WEAPONS AND TACTICS

So far this book may seem like the Frank's RedHot Sauce of presenting—slather that advice on everything! But not all situations are the same. What if you're being asked to do your normal presentation over video or at a conference? What if you don't have PowerPoint and you have to rely on cue cards or, gulp, just your memory? Relax. The principles are the same, but now let's look at how to apply them in other ways.

Set Yourself and Your Audience up for Success

While I wrote this book, a good friend of mine told me about an upcoming talk that he had agreed to deliver to a high school. A teacher had seen him deliver an 11-minute talk at another school and asked him to come into her school and speak at an assembly—for an hour!

He agreed to the talk but was stressing out about it. "I'm struggling to fill my hour with meaningful stuff. How do I keep the attention of hundreds of teenagers for that long?"

My answer was, "You don't." I asked him, "Would you be more comfortable doing thirty minutes?"

"Of course, but I told them I'd do an hour."

"Well, the presentation is still months away. Why not tell them that you'll do a thirty-minute presentation, and that will free up the last thirty minutes for them to have another speaker or do something else of value?"

"Yes! I'm going to call them right now!"

You know your strengths, your material, and what will give your audience the most value. Are you being asked to deliver a four-day instructor course in a day and a half? Are you being asked to give an eight-hour course when four hours would be enough? Your credibility and that of your organization may be on the line. Keep this in mind before you decide to quickly blast through important training or add a bunch of filler just to make an organizer happy.

Stay in Your Lane

There's an old expression, "Jack of all trades, master of none," that refers to someone with a wide knowledge base. This is often used as a compliment, and in most cases, it is. However, when it comes to being a kickass presenter, does your audience expect someone with knowledge that is wide or knowledge that is deep?

You've worked hard to gain expertise in a subject, or maybe even several subjects. You may be asked, and tempted, to present on topics that aren't in your wheelhouse. My advice is to *stay in your lane*, meaning that you stick to talking about topics that you know very well.

A colleague, who is a talented speaker, once told me that he never turns down a speaking gig. "If someone asks me to teach a seminar on swimming, then I better get my butt down to the pool and learn how." All I could think was, "Why would you do that?" You may be able to pull it off, but it's not what you're known for. You're risking your credibility by trying to teach something you know nothing about in exchange for some quick cash.

How to Kick Ass in the Virtual Classroom

Prior to the pandemic of 2020, most presenters couldn't imagine themselves delivering training over video, myself included. But love it or hate it, the virtual classroom is here to stay. This wasn't my specialty, and like many, I had to quickly adapt and learn. Just like presenting in person, it's all about engagement and connecting with your audience. You just have to work harder to make it happen.

Here are my top 10 tips for kickass virtual presentations:

1. *Bring variety and energy.* This isn't your own TV show, and no one wants to watch your talking head for too long, no matter how good you are. Switch things up with snippets of video and conversation with others on the call. Use hand gestures that can be seen on screen.

2. *Trim the fat.* Edit, condense, and shorten. Engagement for online training wanes quicker than in a live session. Can you do a standard one-hour session in 45 minutes? Do it.

3. *Look at your camera.* Eye contact is important for the audience to feel that human connection. Slap a sticky note with an arrow or a smiley face next to the lens to remind you where your gaze should be when you're not scanning your audience.

4. *Raise your camera to eye level.* This is as simple as placing a box or some books under your laptop. No one wants to be looking up from your lap at your double chin and nose hairs.

5. *Encourage participants to have their cameras on.* Tell them why it's in their interest to participate. It'll be more fun and engaging. We are all trained through years of TV and social media to be passive observers of screens, so get the conversation going and trigger people to interact—otherwise, why be live?

6. *Check your lighting.* You're not in the witness protection program, so get some light onto your face. If you need more, try using a

small lamp or a whiteboard to reflect natural light. A visible, lit lamp in the background will make your room feel inviting.

7. *Use a good quality microphone.* Your voice matters. No one cares if you're wearing what you consider to be a dorky headset with a boom mic. What they do care about is hearing your voice. Avoid defaulting to the mic on your laptop. Having the mic that far away from your mouth lets the sound bounce around the room, and the result is tinny, not rich. Oh, and always have a back-up mic ready.

8. *Your background is important.* It gives clues to who you are as a person. Body language expert Mark Bowden says that using a real background instead of a virtual one shows that you're comfortable in your space. That space needs to be clean and tidy. Don't stress over interruptions from kids or pets—it makes you relatable and shows that you're real.

9. *Backstage is in front of you.* Notes and cheat sheets can be mounted behind the camera so that you can keep your eyes up when you glance at them.

10. *Get good with your technology.* Test everything and make sure you're proficient at tasks like screen sharing and switching the host of the meeting. If your presentation is very important or has lots of moving parts (breakout rooms, multimedia, electronic handouts, online testing, polling using an app, etc.) then consider having a competent partner along with you to work those problems while you focus on what you do best—presenting.

Have a plan B for when tech fails. I was participating in some financial training with hundreds of students on the call when breakout rooms— critical to the class—stopped working. The instructor didn't get flustered (at least not outwardly!). His team was on it. They enacted a back-up plan and still delivered effective training.

Total Recall—the Memory Palace Technique

"How in the world does he remember all that?" This was my dad marveling at comedian Ron James, whose comedy is fast paced, verbose, and very poetic.

"I don't know, I guess he knows it because he wrote it?" I replied. I had no idea either.

Flash forward a number of years, and I find myself in a similar situation to Ron, trying to figure out how to remember my own material during a 30-minute comedy set.

There is a technique that I've used often to commit entire presentations to memory, thanks to the book *Moonwalking with Einstein: The Art and Science of Remembering Everything* by Joshua Foer.[81]

Human memory has evolved to keep effortless track of places and emotional events. Think back to your first childhood home. You can easily transport your mind to any room and walk through on your own virtual tour. The *memory palace technique* takes advantage of the fact that we rarely forget spaces like this. Now we just need to put the things or ideas we want to remember in those spaces and then take this little tour in our mind while on stage.

Before you begin you must have your presentation ready to go in final form. Once you start, it becomes very difficult to change course. Break your presentation down into chunks that you can remember with *one idea or key trigger word*. For the sake of demonstration, let's say that this is your list of key words or phrases in order:

1. Your old dog, Bruno
2. The beehive incident
3. McDonald's Hamburglar
4. Printer ink
5. Pumpkin patch

Of course, your list will likely be much longer, but everything else just follows suit.

Pick a location to build the palace, let's say the last house you lived in. Set a route through the house. Perhaps you'll go in through the front door and then work around the main floor clockwise before going upstairs. In your mind, place yourself at the driveway.

1. Imagine that your old dog, Bruno, is 15 feet tall, and he starts happily licking you with his giant tongue the moment you set foot on the property. You can feel the wetness and saliva dripping all over you. You can feel his breath on your wet skin.

2. After a few pets, you push past him only to find a beehive on your front steps. A swarm is loudly buzzing all around, and one of the bees stings you on the elbow. Ouch! You have to step over a dripping honeycomb on your way to the front door.

3. On the front door, there is no handle, just a Hula-Hooped-sized, live Hamburglar face. He opens his mouth to scream, and you have to cram a Big Mac into his gapping maw before the door will open.

4. As you step inside you trip into a kiddie pool filled with blue printer ink. You almost land on top of a naked Nicki Minaj, who is singing and rubbing the ink all over herself.

5. You step out of the pool and into the living room. The floor is soft dirt with pumpkins everywhere! The vines grow quickly and wrap around your ankles, slowing your process.

The trick is to place each item on your list as something vivid to contend with as you walk through your home. The more senses you can engage, the better. Make each experience emotional in some way, be it disgusting, funny, amazing, sexy, or violent. Don't worry—it all stays in the privacy of your own mind! This will take some time to construct, but the investment will be worth it.

As you go through your presentation, you simply walk through your memory palace. You can't get lost. The next critical piece is to rehearse, rehearse, rehearse! Do it in front of a mirror and even other people, using your memory palace as your guide.

This technique has allowed me to confidently deliver speeches and comedy routines without any notes at all. You can also use it to recall anything from exam information to your shopping list.

Playing Your (Cue) Cards Right

What if you've got a speech to deliver and you don't feel confident memorizing it? Cue cards can be a handy way to keep you on track. You can still make hand gestures with them, and they won't tie you to a spot on the stage. Here are a few tips to help you kick ass with cue cards:

1. Make the cards only once you have your talk written out in final draft form. The time to make changes is *before* you make up cue cards.
2. Choose cards that are 5" x 7" or smaller. Otherwise, you may as well be using entire sheets of paper, which are distracting to both you and your audience.
3. Write only on one side. If the color of the side facing the audience roughly matches your wardrobe, they will be less noticeable.
4. Number your cards so that you don't need to staple or bind them together.
5. No sentences! Just like slides, cards provide a quick handrail for you to glance at. Write your key trigger words in large font using a felt pen.
6. Include important numbers, dates, or other content that you want to be certain of getting right.
7. Rehearse with your cards! Rehearse until you don't need them anymore. By this point you should have mastered your content, and the cards will just be there as a safety net. Like carrying bear spray on a hike, if all goes well, you won't need it at all.

Copresenting

What about presenting with another person? On the face of it, this sounds like a great idea because there's less work. If you're not sure what you're doing, your copresenter can always pick up the slack, right? Not necessarily. It didn't work during your high school group assignment, and this is no different.

Why would you copresent? Perhaps you worked on a project with someone else, or multiple people, and you've all been asked to speak about it. Maybe you're learning to teach a class, so you start out by coteaching with the current instructor.

The downside is that you're introducing more variables, and you'll need even more rehearsal time to ensure smooth transitions.

On the upside, you're bringing more expertise and experience to the presentation, and the audience will get more novelty and variety with two or more speakers. Your copresenter can also be there to troubleshoot tech issues and to provide you with valuable feedback.

Here are my tips for rocking a joint presentation:

1. Both presenters must *master the content of the entire presentation.* If one person has to cancel at the last minute, the show must go on. That's hard to pull off if you only know your half.
2. Avoid clumsy transitions by *rehearsing* them. Some presentations will require that you bounce back and forth often, while others will just have presenters switching at natural pauses, like during a break.
3. Rehearse your opening and closing. Who is starting off, and how will each of you be introduced?
4. When you're not speaking, get out of the way. This means moving to where you are no longer in the audience's eyeline. As a new instructor, I was sharing the stage with another speaker whom I

had not worked with before and whom I really didn't know. As I was speaking, he stayed at the front of the room, sat down, and read a newspaper! (I get that I'm dating myself here.) There was no subtle way for me to address this, so I let it go and talked with him about it at a break. Never again!

5. Check your ego. Even if your copresenter is amazing, they likely won't do it the way you'd would do it. This can be frustrating, but there are many ways to be effective at the same job.

Presenting at Conferences

I admit it: I'm a conference nerd. I've had a ton of cool experiences and met some incredible people, all because I made the investment in time and money to go. Whether they are for hostage negotiators or hypnotists, I love the atmosphere, the learning, and the free snacks. (See how I snuck in the rule of three there?)

Conferences are a great way to reach a wide audience with your message and to gain experience and credibility. They are also a perfect place to network and to see how others present. Many industries have annual conferences that are held at a national or international level. They often consist of some bigger keynote speakers for all attendees at once and a number of breakout sessions for smaller groups.

Industry conferences may not pay presenters but will often offer other perks, like waving the conference fee. Though they may have the budget to pay some professional keynote speakers, you'll likely have to pay for your own expenses. "What? No limo from the airport?!"

A question to ask yourself first is, "Why put in all the work to present?" Hopefully it's because you've got an important message and maybe even some awesome, cutting-edge stuff to teach others. Expectations are high at conferences, and you really want to aim to hit it out of the park.

Whenever you can, *attend the entire event.* Some speakers just slide in for their talk and are gone again, and they miss a great opportunity to network, develop relationships, and keep their fingers on the pulse of the industry. Sticking around, especially after your talk, gives attendees a chance to speak with you, ask questions, and build relationships that can be mutually beneficial for years to come.

Often you will have to apply to speak at these events up to eight months in advance. Most will require a minimum of an instructor biography, a course title, and a short description of the course objective. Typically, whatever you send in with your application will also appear on the conference website and app and may be printed in a booklet for distribution at the event.

Here are a few tips that will not only increase your odds of being chosen to speak but will also help put bums on seats at your presentation:

Create a catchy title. Keep in mind that attendees may have a huge selection of presentations to choose from in any given time slot, so you want your title to stand out. Imagine you're attending a conference for emergency communications officers—you know, the people who answer when you call 911. Which presentation would you rather see: "A Functional Review of Interoperability—The Sustainable Model," or "Cybersecurity—Are You Putting Your Call Center at Risk?" Your title should say something about your talk but also pique people's interest to at least read more about you and your topic.

Avoid using the word "theory," especially in the title. This is a one-way ticket to Snoozeville. Try to think of a riveting title that includes the word theory—go ahead, I'll wait. The Theory of Sex? Nope. Don't give prospective audience members any reason to file your presentation under "boring."

Create an engaging course description. What are people going to learn and take away from your presentation? Put this information near the start of your description. You may want to lead with a question that will get the reader thinking. For example, "The United States had 612 mass shootings in 2020—the highest number on record.[82] Do you know what to do if this happens at your workplace? Are you prepared to take action? This powerful presentation will showcase some important incidents from North America and around the world. You may find yourself at the front end of one of these events and will benefit from understanding the changing trends in offender behavior, police training, and citizen response." Granted, this example is more provocative than most. Regardless, let the audience know what's in it for them. Do the work for them by telling them up front why they should care.

Submit your biography and above all, be honest! The quickest way to flush your credibility down the toilet is to lie and embellish who you are and what you've done. You don't need guru status in your industry to draw people into your presentation, so keep it real. Ensure that what you say about yourself relates not only to your topic, but also to your audience. If you're speaking about how to develop clients in the oil and gas industry, then keep to relevant experience, education, successes, and industry credentials. No one cares that you enjoy long walks on the beach or that you teach water aerobics in your spare time. Write in the third person: "Katherine Watson has worked in the nonprofit sector for over 16 years …"

At the conference, be prepared by knowing exactly what room you'll be speaking in and what to expect in terms of the room arrangement and the setup of the lighting, microphone, laptop, screen, flip charts, etc. Pry yourself away from the hospitality suite or free swag at the trade show, and go check this out well before your time slot.

Get to your speaking room early and get set up as soon as possible. This will give you the maximum amount of time to troubleshoot any little issues (and there are always issues) and to greet people at the door as they come in. This small gesture will help you to convey warmth and presence. As people meet you, they are also less likely to sit way at the back of the room!

Never go over time. This is a sin for any presentation, but especially at conferences where schedules are tight. If there are multiples rooms, often there's only a 10-minute break between presentations, and a lot has to happen in that time. Audience members will flood the halls trying to find what room they need to be in next, while also hitting the bathroom and topping up their coffee. For presenters it's even worse. The next speaker will be salivating like a retriever in a duck blind, ready to swoop in and begin their setup. When you've finished your presentation, be ready to grab your stuff and get out of their way.

Case Study Presentation Guide

Case studies are used to impart lessons to an audience that were learned through a real-life event. These are very common in law enforcement, military, firefighting, and disaster response, for example. Perhaps you worked as part of a disaster recovery team that was first on the ground after a forest fire? Maybe you traveled to Africa to build wells in a remote community? Now others are asking to hear your story, perhaps at an industry event or conference. Where do you start?

First, identify the *learning objectives* or *takeaways* that you want the audience to leave with. These "lessons learned" can be touched on as they come up in the presentation and then recapped at the end.

A case study used as a presentation should, above all else, *tell a story*. This means quality pictures, audio clips, maps, diagrams, props, and video if available. Nothing kills a good story like low-quality media.

Next, *set the context*. In a conference environment, you'll likely be telling this story to people who are not from your city (or even your country) and may even be from outside your industry. This means laying the groundwork by painting a picture of the who, what, when, where, and why of your story.

For example, if you're talking about your city, what size is it? How large is your company, center, or agency? How are people deployed? What training did they have? How many people were working that day? Remember to continually look at your presentation from the perspective of an outsider. You may need to explain some industry terms or jargon or simply use common language. Because we often do this without even recognizing it (the curse of knowledge), a good test is to present to someone who wasn't there and doesn't know much about your topic.

Tell the story in *chronological order*, and allow it to unfold the way it happened. I recall a case study at a conference for hostage negotiators that was presented by a team of three people who all played different roles in the incident. Near the beginning of their two-hour presentation, one speaker couldn't help spilling the catastrophic end to their story. Not only did this obviously surprise and annoy the other presenters, but it confused the audience and ruined the experience of the story.

Give the audience the *same amount of information* to work with that you had at the time. This takes them on a journey with you and allows them to ask themselves the question, What would I have done at that point? You may even want to pose some questions along the way: "What would you have done here? What should our priorities be at this point? What are we missing?"

Tell the story from a *human perspective*. Were you scared at points? Tired? Hungry? Injured? Confused? Paint a vivid and emotional picture, and let the audience experience the event through another human being's eyes.

Be candid and honest. If you did something well, was it due to good luck or good tactics? What allowed you to succeed? What processes did you follow that worked well or failed? If you failed or could have done something better, then admit it. Talk about what you've learned and what is being done to correct the shortfall.

Keep it tight. It's easy to get off on entertaining (to you) tangents, but are they relevant to your audience and the story?

Wrap it up in a nice bow at the end. What happened in the aftermath? Did the perpetrator end up in jail? If so, for how long? Did people recover from their injuries? Where are they now? What changes were made? Use news stories, articles, and pictures. Anticipate what questions people might have, and look to answer them during the presentation. Once again, test this on people who are not familiar with your topic, and have them identify the open loops that need to be closed.

Chapter Takeaways

1. Use your presenting time wisely. Do you need all the time you have been given? Do you need more?
2. Presenting over video makes engagement tougher but engagement is still possible through the purposeful use of eye contact, hand gestures, and interaction with your audience.
3. Use the memory palace technique to memorize your entire presentation.
4. Cue cards can be effective—just remember to rehearse with them!
5. Copresenting can be challenging—to get good, the key is to rehearse together.
6. When presenting at a conference
    a. attend the entire event,
    b. create a catchy presentation title,
    c. in the course description, tell your audience what they will learn and why they should care,
    d. keep your biography honest and relevant,
    e. know where to go and get there early, and
    f. never go over time.
7. For a case study, set the context, tell it in chronological order, be human, be honest, and don't leave the audience with questions.

Exercise

Build a memory palace for something mundane, like a shopping list. Use it to gain confidence so that you can rock your next no-notes presentation.

Take a critical look at one of your existing presentations to see if the audience would benefit from it being longer or shorter. If you were going to present this at a conference, what title and course description would you choose?

Chapter 8

LESS BITTER, MORE GLITTER

"In other centuries, human beings wanted to be
saved, or improved, or freed, or educated. But
in our century, they want to be entertained."

—Michael Crichton[83]

Don't be boring. Great advice for presenters ... but how do we do that?
It's good to have a trick or two in your repertoire to mix things up and
set yourself apart from the average. When you're an audience member, it's
hard to be disengaged when you're having fun.

Candies, Magic, Props, and Music

If you were hosting a get-together, you'd likely put on some music and lay
out some food and drinks—so why not here? What's stopping you from
offering a few snacks in a bowl at the back, such as granola bars or fruit?
Why can't you play music? If there's no cafeteria, why can't you have some
bottled water or juice boxes? Use your imagination and think about what
you've enjoyed at other presentations. Here are a few ways to add some
sparkle that you might not have thought of.

Candies for participation. As I mentioned in the section on questions
in chapter 6, during some presentations I'll bring candies to hand out
as a reward for participation, answering questions, or winning in-class

competitions. Giving something also tends to invoke a sense of reciprocity with your audience—they're getting something from you, so they feel obligated to give something back. In this case all you want back from them is their attention and participation.

The Coloring Book of Magic. This book is set up so that if you flip through the pages one way, the pages appear to be empty. The next time you flip through, they have the outlines of cartoons on them. The third time, the cartoons are colored in. It's a simple trick that leaves people puzzled and, more importantly, paying attention.

I explain it like this: Starting out as a presenter, you don't have much to go on and your skills are like these pages—blank (flip blank pages). As you learn and gain experience, some pictures start to take shape (flip outlined pages). My expectation of anyone presenting at the end of this workshop is that you're at least here (flip colored pages). What we should all be striving for is to be as complete and as colorful as possible.

As childish as magic can be, adults still seem to love it. The important part, just like when telling jokes, is that you *relate it to your message* and *do it well.*

Props help make the abstract more tangible and concrete. A physical item is often better than a picture of the item. Props can also help make analogies stick. Have a look at your presentation for places where a prop might fit. Take a wander through a toy store, a magic shop, a costume shop, or a dollar store. Take note of other presenters and where, when, and how they use props.

Consider adding some music. When we think of presentations, we don't often associate them with music. But why not? Research in 2011 by Ronald A. Berk of Johns Hopkins University showed that "music embedded throughout a PowerPoint presentation can sustain attention, while slipping the content into long-term memory."[84] Music taps into both hemispheres of the brain. Research by Chris Brewer in 1995 showed that even passive background music can increase attention levels, improve retention and memory, extend focused learning time, and expand thinking skills. [85] On top of all this, music creates *mood!* What mood are you going for?

Music before Your Presentation

Playing good music as the audience enters can be a way to start engaging even before you start speaking. It's important that the music is relatable to your audience. If you're about to speak at a seniors' home on the topic of … well just about anything … maybe Wu Tang Clan isn't the best choice. If you're speaking to a high school or university audience, make sure your music is fresh. Playing songs that hit their peak three years ago will make you seem out of touch. I like to bring a small Bluetooth speaker that is independent of the presentation. This allows me to play music from my phone while setting up everything else.

Music during the Presentation

There are some quiet times where music might be appropriate, like when audience members are writing or working in small groups. Music can help fill the reflective silence and keep the energy where you want it.

During a presentation I give on persuasion techniques, I use an example from one my favorite childhood TV shows—*CHiPs*. It ran from 1977 to 1983 and followed the adventures of Frank Poncherello and Jon Baker, two motorcycle officers from the California Highway Patrol. This was back in the day when every TV show had its own theme song and intro. I could have just talked about the show, but that's boring. In the presentation I first play the theme music and see who can guess the show. The Gen Xers in the room always love the short walk down memory lane.

Memes as a Preshow

Rather than just your title slide being up on the screen for 20 minutes before you start, try a looping meme slideshow. I like to use ones that relate to the audience and don't require much reading. I gather them from social media and keep them in a folder throughout the year. Most elicit a quick chuckle with a five- to seven-second exposure, and you can set your presentation to loop back around at the end.

Energizers

Sometimes you just need to liven things up. Maybe the audience has been sitting all day, the next break isn't for 45 minutes, and you don't have any small-group activities coming up. It's handy to have an energizer or two that you can pull out of your back pocket to change the energy in the room. I get it—some people hate this stuff! No one wants to look like an idiot playing silly games, so choose your audience and activity wisely. I prefer energizers that don't require any props or prep work and that can be done in under a few minutes.

If you can, tie a lesson from your energizer activity back to your message. One great way to do this is to use the *reflect and share* and *teach back* reviews in the next chapter as energizers.

Music or Dance Break

What? I'm not going to have my audience dance! The first time I experienced this was at a conference for police instructors—and it worked really well. This is for when you've got a slump in energy and the audience would benefit from getting their blood pumping a little. I've used these to great effect—it reenergizes your audience and gets a few smiles. The key is that you must take the lead.

The Race. Put on some great upbeat music and ask the audience to stand. Their feet stay planted shoulder-width apart. Have them put one hand on their cheek and the other hand on their other cheek (butt cheek!). Have them switch hands a couple of times so that their arms are doing the motion as if they were running. Next have them imagine that they're going to run a race to the end of the block against their 10-year-old nephew, and there's no way they're going to lose. Say "Go!" and have them sprint—just with their arms—for about 10 seconds. That's it. What I like about this is that it only takes about 30 seconds, start to finish, and then you're back on track.

Rock, Paper, Scissors Tournament

Just as it sounds. Have people pair up and play a best of three. The loser must then become part of the cheer squad as the winner advances until there are only two players left and the rest of the audience is cheering for their player. Even with a large group, you can get through this in minutes. Bonus marks if you can tie it into your message!

A kickass twist on this is to replace the hand gestures with full body gestures called cowboy, ninja, grizzly. Players start standing back-to-back. On the count of three, they both jump, turn to face each other, and assume a pose. The cowboy has a finger gun in each hand as if they've just drawn them from a holster on either hip. The ninja assumes a martial arts stance with both hands in a karate chop position in front of them. The grizzly has both hands up like claws. Grizzly beats cowboy, ninja beats grizzly (think samurai sword), and cowboy beats ninja (don't bring a knife to a gun fight).

Chapter Takeaways

Little extras like props, music, magic, candy, and pauses to energize the audience can set you apart from the average by making your presentation entertaining, engaging, and memorable.

Exercise

Take a look at a presentation you deliver to see where you may be able to introduce some music, even if it's only while the audience is filling the room.

Chapter 9

THAT'LL LEARN 'EM

"So, what did you learn in school today?" I asked almost daily as the kids dumped their backpacks on the floor and headed for the fridge.

"Nothing." Their enthusiasm was electric.

"Really? You just spent eight hours at school and learned nothing?"

Of course, they likely learned something, but digging through their minds for an example and explaining it at that point was hopeless. How can we make sure this doesn't happen after people leave one of your presentations?

What Have They Learned?

Coach John Wooden famously said, "You haven't taught until they've learned."[86] But how will you know that what you've presented will be retained and used later? One great way is to *ask your audience*. After a section of material, or at the end of your presentation, have audience members reflect on key concepts and answer a few questions on paper:

Reflect.

1. What is significant about what you just learned?
2. How will you apply this knowledge?
3. Who would benefit from what you've learned and how will you share it?

After this reflection, you can choose to go further, with sharing or teaching back (see below).

Share. Now have audience members pair up and share their answers with a partner. This builds in some accountability to actually do the assignment and allows them to see how others will employ what they've learned.

Teach back. Have audience members choose a concept that they just learned and explain it in simple terms to a partner. This allows them to reflect on new concepts and then put them into their own words. It serves as more repetition of the material and forces them to think about it from the aspect of teaching it to someone else.

Tell them how much time they will have to complete this exercise, and then walk around among the group and see how they're doing. If you haven't given them a specific amount of time, you'll know it's time to bring it back when there is a dip in the volume of the room.

When the group is back together, ask audience members to share their insights. If you're midpresentation, you might only ask for a few of these. At the end of a longer session, like a full day, it's worthwhile getting a response from each person (provided the group isn't too big).

I've attended training where this was used first thing in the morning during a weeklong course. Each student shared an "A-ha!" moment from the day before, which was a great way to reinforce what was taught up to that point.

Here are some more possible questions for the end of the session:

1. What is the key takeaway for you?
2. What were you surprised to learn?
3. What concepts do you think are most valuable or useful?
4. What was the least valuable and why?
5. How will you specifically apply these concepts?

6. Who will you share these concepts with?

7. Who will you contact to keep you accountable for implementing this learning?

Fun and Games as a Review

Everyone loves a good game. If you can introduce a little competition, even better. I *bring prizes* for the top teams. This might be anything from chocolate bars to swag I've picked up at an industry trade show. Props like buzzers and music make it even more engaging.

Games are a great way to sneak in a review of a presentation without a standard, boring, Q&A–style review. This can be done before a written exam or on its own to go over key concepts one last time. Because we want our audience to have to recall the answers, don't let them use their notes or any handouts. Otherwise, this just turns into an exercise of who can find the answer in their notes the quickest. Here are some that I like:

Jeopardy. There are many easy-to-use PowerPoint templates for Jeopardy where all you need to do is plug in your questions and answers. What questions should you use? Go back to your learning objectives. It's fun to throw in some quirky or obscure questions as well to mix things up. Divide the group into teams and have them choose a team name. Have the teams sit together in their groups to keep everyone organized.

A great way to kick this game up a notch is to add in a *Nerf dart competition*. Before a team can answer a question, they must send someone up the front of the room to knock over an empty soda can with a foam dart from single-shot Nerf gun. Place a can for each team on a table and have them shoot from behind another table or a line taped on the floor about 10 feet away. Each team can be named after their brand of sugary drinks, and it only counts when they knock down their own cans. I have yet to run a class that doesn't love this game.

Some other alternatives to Jeopardy are inspired by TV game shows, like *Family Feud* and *Are You Smarter than a Fifth Grader?* Free templates are easily downloadable for each.

SWAT Team. This one I learned from a seminar with police trainer Richard Neil Sr. Students love it. It gets very physical, so you'll want to make sure you've got the right group, in the right attire, and in a room that will accommodate it.

Start by writing out the answers to your review questions on standard-sized sticky notes. You'll need at least 20–30 of them. Stick them all over a wall in a room that can be mostly cleared of furniture. Divide the students into teams, and give each team a fly swatter (these are easy to get from a dollar store). Place a taped line on the floor across the room from your answer wall. The idea is that none of the students can read the answers on the sticky notes from behind the line. Divide the class into four or five teams. Each team chooses a representative to do the swatting and that person changes with each question. Pose the question and then yell, "GO!" The "swatters" will run to the answer wall, and the first person to get their swatter on the right sticky note gets the points. Warning: this is a great game for students like police recruits or others who are in reasonable shape and don't mind some physical contact. This game can get a little rowdy, but everyone has a ton of fun.

60-Second Countdown. This can be done as a review or even as a quick energizer partway through the presentation. Put the audience into two or three teams, each with a flip chart or whiteboard. When the clock starts, each team must send one person up to the board to write down as many key concepts or words from the presentation as the group can remember (without their notes). The group with the longest list wins. This can be done as a group, with each team shouting their answers to the person writing, or individually, where each person on the team goes up in turn with the marker being passed to the next member.

Color Jenga. You can purchase Jenga towers with different colors already painted on them, or even paint your own. (This also works with the standard wooden Jenga blocks.) These sets come with a die that has the different colors on it. Have teams answer a question. If they get it right, they roll the die and pull the corresponding-colored block from the stack. An alternative is to put questions into color categories and have them choose. The team with the most blocks when the tower falls wins. Incorporate two or more Jenga stacks to make it more interesting.

Trasketball. Group the class into teams. Ask a question and have the students write down their answer. Choose a person to answer. (Alternatively, have one member from each team write their answer on a whiteboard). If they are correct, they get to toss a ball into a trash can to earn points for their team. They can choose to shoot from behind a one-point line or from a line further back for two points. You can use wadded pieces of paper or soft/squishy balls from a dollar store. For a net, you can use either a trash can or get fancy with a special one that even looks like a basketball hoop and net.

Teams earn points that win them prizes. An alternative to this is to use Velcro darts/balls on a dartboard, foam Nerf darts fired at a target or pop can ... you get the idea.

You can use a list of questions that you hold onto or reveal them on a screen or whiteboard one by one.

Evaluating Your Training

Before we get into feedback and testing, it's worth understanding why we do it and where it fits into the training process. *The Kirkpatrick evaluation model* was developed in the 1950s by Professor Donald Kirkpatrick at the University of Wisconsin. It's a four-level approach to help measure the effectiveness of any training:

Level 1—Reaction (Feedback)

Did the learners enjoy the presentation and think that it was valuable, relevant, and useful? This is typically measured through feedback forms and even discussion with the audience members.

You should seek the audience's reaction to all your presentations. We'll get into feedback in a moment, but realize that it doesn't have to be a formal process. Talk to audience members afterward and ask for their candid feedback. If they didn't like the presentation or didn't feel that it was valuable, it's unlikely that it'll result in the behavior change you're looking to elicit in them.

I once attended a mandatory presentation by a work colleague. I heard grumbling from coworkers who had attended previous sessions, but I went with an open mind. Most of the presentation was ok, but my team thought that one part in particular was everything from a complete waste of time to downright insulting. The presenter didn't ask for feedback, so I reached out in an email with my thoughts, including specifics on what we found valuable and why. I also gave feedback on what the team didn't like, why they didn't like it, and what the presenter might change to make it more effective.

The presenter's response was that we were wrong—that the entire presentation was very valuable, and she wouldn't be changing a thing. Here's the kicker—she had more than 30 of these sessions left to go! She felt that it was better to carry on than to make a change to improve the presentation. This is like being on a hike in the woods, being told you're going in the wrong direction, and continuing anyway.

Your audience gets to decide what is of value to them. If you still feel that what you are presenting is worthwhile, then maybe you need to reevaluate how you're delivering it and double down on the audience's "what's in it for me" factor—like showing real-life examples of why it's important, why it works, and why they should buy in.

Level 2—Learning (Testing)

Did the training meet the learning objectives? To know the answer to this, we measure the knowledge and skills students have obtained through testing, projects, exercises, etc.

Most one-time presentations will not require this level of evaluation. For example, a two-hour presentation at a conference likely doesn't need a test, whereas a full-day corporate training session may. If what you are teaching is a physical skill—say, how to juggle chainsaws or how to apply a tourniquet—then a practical test should be included.

Level 3—Behavior

Did the presentation or training cause a change in the work product after the training ended? This is tougher to measure but can be done well after the presentation through supervisor observations, customer feedback, and self-assessment questionnaires.

Evaluating behavior change is beyond the scope of this book as most presentations, short of multiday training courses, will not require this level of evaluation. The same goes for level 4.

Level 4—Results

Did the training produce tangible results and a return on investment? This can be measured through things like employee retention, reduced costs, quality improvement, customer satisfaction, and increased sales.

The Hotwash

The origin of the term "hotwash" is hard to pin down, but it has come to mean a quick and dirty debrief that occurs immediately after an event. Legendary speaker and author Brian Tracy attributes much of his success to some important hotwash questions he asks himself at the end of each speaking event:[87]

1. What did I do well?
2. What would I do differently?

Ask yourself these questions while the event is fresh in your mind, and *write down your answers*. Make as long a list of answers as possible for each question. Did your slide deck run smoothly? Did an important story have the audience on the edge of their seats? Did that joke you tried out get any smiles? *Be specific*. Once you have it captured, you can relax knowing that you can pull out the list later and make whatever changes you need to be more effective next time.

> "Feedback is the breakfast of champions."
>
> —Ken Blanchard[88]

So ... Did They Like It?

Do you consider yourself to be an above-average driver? Most people do, but what is this opinion based on? We can't all be above average! If you could accurately test everyone's driving ability, the results would fall nicely onto a bell curve—meaning that half of the drivers out there are *below average*. Why? Because after some introductory lessons and their road test, few people ever get any further feedback on their driving skills (other than maybe the odd one-finger wave from other drivers). Feedback is essential because we are sometimes poor judges of our own performance.

It's Hard to Read the Label When You're inside the Bottle

When I was training to race in the Ironman triathlon (3.8 km swim, 180 km bike, and 42.2 km run) I went to a training camp put on by professional triathletes. To improve our swimming, they had us all swim a number of lengths of the pool while a trainer with cameras on a pole walked beside us on the deck. One camera captured what we were doing below the water and one above. We then reviewed the video: the results were stunning.

Most swimmers didn't recognize themselves, and some even argued with the instructors that the person on the screen couldn't possibly be them. One guy said, "I don't kick like that! I don't do that thing with my arms!" Like it or not, the video didn't lie.

So how do you know what level your presentation skills are at? The answer lies in getting meaningful feedback from everyone you can, especially from truly good presenters. Videotaping and reviewing your presentation is also hugely valuable. Trust me, it can be hard to watch! Some people can't even stand the sound of their own voice. I don't know anyone who enjoys this, but the point here is to look at what you do and how you do it with the goal of being better next time.

Get Better Feedback through Evaluation Forms

It's the end of a training session, and the presenter hands you an evaluation form. You look at the paper and pray it doesn't require much writing. You check a bunch of boxes giving the presenter "five out of five" in all categories, hand it in, and get the heck outta there.

Sound familiar? The presenter thumbs through them, sees a bunch of "fives," and walks out of the room with a head swollen like a 40-lb M&M. Who does this serve?

Here are some ways to get a more accurate evaluation:

1. Have the students complete short-answer and open-ended questions as opposed to circling a number on a scale or checking a box. This will force them to articulate what they thought and why. Here are some that have worked well for me:

    a. Please identify what you consider to be the strengths of this training.

    b. Please identify the area(s) where the presentation could be improved.

    c. How will you use this learning going forward?

2. Hand the evaluation sheet out at the start of the class. Ask the audience to fill it in as they go, and remind them throughout the session.

3. Build in enough time to fill out the evaluation. If you hand the form out with only five minutes left in the session, audience members feel pressured, and the quality of their answers suffers.

4. Collect the evaluation forms *before* your closing remarks. Let everyone know that this isn't all that is left in the session. Once again, this will prevent audience members from rushing through the form so that they can leave. Once you've collected them all, you can close with something purposeful.

Reading my course evaluations can be soul crushing. It might be 98% positive, but I tend to dwell on the 2% that isn't. Sometimes that negative bit of feedback is just a one-off, but sometimes it will shine light into a blind spot you didn't even know you had. Though we hope for nothing but glowing reviews, the real lessons come from failure. Sometimes you kick ass. Sometimes you learn.

Feedback forms can also be a great source of testimonials to use to promote your presentation in the future.

This Is Only a Test

Some presentations will benefit from a written test. Telling the audience that there will be a written test at the end often makes people pay more attention and take better notes.

Here's why you'd want to have one:

1. It confirms learning. If you want to know if your audience can recall what you just presented (at least in the short term), a test will tell you. It also provides important feedback for your future presentations. If everyone struggles with a particular question, for example, maybe the problem isn't them. Look at how you're presenting and reviewing the information and how it's worded in the test.

2. It reinforces what you have taught. As we discussed in chapter 4 on making learning stick, a test is just another opportunity to recall the information, which makes the learning more robust. The key here is to use a recall test (like fill in the blanks or short answer) vs. a recognition test (like multiple choice).

3. It can add legitimacy to your training through an identifiable metric. Those paying the bill want a return on their investment. A written test can help to prove that this isn't just a fun session away from "real" work.

What Do I Include in a Test?

You already know what's important—go back to your objectives and ensure that you are touching on all of them in the questions you ask. If you are writing a new presentation, consider creating the test as soon as you're happy with the objectives. You should have at least one question or task for each objective.

Testing can take us down a rabbit hole that I won't go into here. Developing a test that is both valid and reliable is a challenge for almost anyone. Here is my advice: Look at what the audience needs to know or needs to be able to perform later and *test them in a way that resembles how they will be asked to use it in the real world.*

Having them regurgitate a list of actions is not as good as asking them to explain how, why, and when they will take these actions. For example, let's say you're presenting on workplace safety. It's good that students can list the different types of fire extinguishers available, but is this truly useful in the real world?

Perhaps a better question would be like this: "You are heading to a job site where your main fire hazard will be electrical. Before you choose an extinguisher to take with you, what are you looking for on the extinguisher's label to know if it will be useful?" This is a short-answer question that forces the student to recall the information.

Consequences

So, what if someone fails the test? This is something you need to have worked out ahead of time. The real question is, how important is this information or skill? Is it something that an employee critically needs to know to be able to do the job? If it is, you'll also have to sort out how to remediate the problem by building more teaching time for that student and scheduling a retest.

When I worked as an instructor in police tactics, the skills I was teaching involved complex decision-making under stress, which sometimes had life-or-death consequences. This created some real dilemmas when a student didn't pass a test, and there were many people and processes involved to ensure that a standard was kept.

Likely the real-world implications of whatever you're presenting on won't be so dramatic. In most of my presentations, the test is simply used as another opportunity for the audience to recall the material. Most of the objectives aren't critical, and the material can be looked up later.

Depending on the presentation I'll often *introduce some competition* into the written exam. I'll reward speed and accuracy by awarding prizes for the first three or five people who turn in their tests *and* who have a perfect score. All you need to do is to number them as they come in.

I prefer to have students switch tests with each other so that we can go over it as a group rather than collecting them and doing it myself later. This is just another opportunity to see the material again and to talk about issues that come up.

Let's Bring It in for a Landing

"*Where might the smallest change make the biggest difference?*" This is a question that I heard trainer and author Brian Willis ask live. Looking at a book like this in its entirety might just overwhelm you into inaction. Start small. Make one change that will get you a quick win—and then just keep winning.

One way to become a better presenter and teacher is to *become a student again*. When you reach a certain level of comfort or mastery in a subject, it's easy to forget what it's like to be new. I ran smack into this when I left law enforcement for the financial industry. I traded my black belt for a white belt, and the learning curve was steep.

Of course, you don't have to change careers to experience this (in fact, please don't!). Take a class in something you know nothing about. Pay close attention to how the instructors deliver the material—now you're taking two classes at the same time. When you're there, *be the student that you would want in your class*. Show up early, be prepared, sit up front, take notes, engage in activities, and ask questions.

Presenting Is a Great Privilege

You owe it to your audience to bring the best you have and to provide them with value. At the start of a week of intense training, I was once told by an excellent instructor, Hans Marrero (USMC Ret.), "We only have so many days on this earth. I am choosing to spend this day with you, and you with me. This is a day that you and I will never get back. I promise not to waste your time." He certainly did not.

Now, go forth and kick some ass!

Chapter Takeaways

1. You can quickly find out if the audience is learning through an in-class exercise involving reflection, sharing, and teach-backs.
2. Punch up your presentation review by incorporating games and competition.
3. Some presentations will benefit from a test, which can build practice in using your learning objectives.
4. Conduct your own hotwash by asking yourself what went well and what you would do differently.
5. Seek feedback at every opportunity.
6. Done correctly, evaluation forms can be a great way to collect feedback.

Exercises

Open up one of your current presentations. Would your audience benefit from an in-class review, a review game, or a written test based around your learning objectives? If so, how much presentation time do you have to dedicate to this? With the time you do have, what would give you the most bang for your buck? Have a look at your objectives, and create a review or test for your next session.

What are you doing to seek feedback from your presentations? Create a note on your phone or a page in a notebook to use for a hotwash immediately after your next presentation.

RESOURCES

Slide Checklist

Now that you've built some slides, you can go through each one and make sure that they meet some basic criteria:

1. The takeaway message is the focus of the slide (one idea per slide).
2. Your image is sharp and helps explain your idea.
3. Text is
   a. limited (do you even need any?),
   b. easy to see (in a large font, in colors that stand out, and in the upper half of the slide), and
   c. not just the title—the text *is* your message.

Presentation Checklist

You've looked over your slides and are happy with them. Now it's time to take a broader view of your presentation and slide deck.

1. You've memorized your purposeful opener.
2. Your identified objectives are met.
3. Your takeaway messages are clear.
4. You've used the FASST acronym (at least in part) to ensure that your ideas are sticky.
   a. Feelings
   b. Analogies
   c. Surprise
   d. Stories
   e. Tangible
5. You've injected humor.

6. You've built in a review to cover your objectives (if appropriate).

7. Video and audio run smoothly.

8. You've memorized your purposeful close.

Equipment Checklist

1. Have your entire presentation ready to go on a *flash drive* in case your laptop crashes.

2. Have your *laptop* ready to go in case the venue's computer crashes.

3. Have a *presentation remote* (with a back-up and extra batteries). A kickass presenter can't be handcuffed to the computer. This is a small investment with a huge payoff.

4. Bring any *adapter cables* you might need—for example, HDMI to VGA.

5. An *extension cord and power bar* are very handy.

6. A *small, high-quality speaker* can do a great job. Don't rely entirely on the venue's sound system.

7. If you need internet access, make sure you have a back-up plan, like turning your phone into a *Wi-Fi hotspot*.

8. Have *your entire presentation printed out* so that if all else fails, you can go without technology.

9. Remember *props*, handouts, games, extra dry-erase markers, and any other odds and sods.

Room Setup Checklist

1. *Test your presentation*—screen, projector, sound, video, and presentation remote. This always takes more time than you think it will.

2. *Teaching aids*—get the flip chart where you want it, have working whiteboard markers in the right spot, and set any props where you need them.

3. *Lighting*—can the audience see you from everywhere in the room? You are the presentation, not what's on the screen. Next, can they

clearly see your screen from everywhere, especially at the back? Does the audience have enough light to be able to take notes?

4. *Seating*—this might be something you can't change, like in an auditorium. If you've got a small class, you can move the desks, chairs, and tables into the configuration you like. Maybe you'll use a hollow square where you can easily interact with each audience member or perhaps table groups that will be better for small-group work.

5. *Remove clutter and distractions*—that flip chart with stuff from another class, the piles of paper and extra pens, even your own laptop bag and props. Tuck it all away so that the audience can focus on you.

6. *Check yourself*—before you wreck yourself! Is your phone where you want it, and is it on silent?

ACKNOWLEDGMENTS

Who knew writing a book would be challenging? I didn't get here on my own, and I am grateful for so many people. Here's a small list:

My wife, Connie, for your unyielding support for my dreams and this daunting project.

Brian Willis for your mentorship in so many areas of life and for inspiring me to strive for excellence.

Matt Blair for challenging me to take this path of training trainers.

My Book Launchers team: Roy Rocha, Julie Broad, John Schlimm, Nicole Larson, and many more behind the scenes ... I would be lost without you.

My inspiring police trainers at the Calgary Police Service's Skills & Procedures Unit. You set a high bar early in my career: Darren Leggatt, Mike Starchuk, Gary Stoney, Chris Butler, and Wally Muller.

My friends and colleagues who gave me and this book their time, skill, and energy: Derrick Shirley, Rebecca Hanna, John Warin, and Sharon Koch.

Peter Pecksen for the photos and friendship.

Brett Forte for continually giving me opportunities in comedy I didn't yet earn.

My parents, Marcel and Diana Fraser, for a lifetime of love, support, and encouragement.

Erin Skye Kelly for helping me to define a dream and to Stu Hughes for pushing me way out of my comedy comfort zone.

James and Nichole Budd for your enduring friendship and expertise.

Bill Marsh and the excellent instructors at the Southern Alberta Institute of Technology photography program for helping me see the world through a different lens.

Dr. Terry D. Anderson from the School of Criminology and Criminal Justice at the University of the Fraser Valley in Abbotsford, BC. You helped me define my life's purpose, and here I am decades later, collecting wisdom and using it to empower others.

The incredible trainers, colleagues, and friends I have made through the International Law Enforcement Educators and Trainers Association (ILEETA)—iron sharpens iron.

RECOMMENDED READING

Books

Brown, Brené. 2015. *Daring Greatly: How the Courage to Be Vulnerable Transforms the Way We Live, Love, Parent, and Lead.* New York: Avery.

Brown, Peter C., Henry L. Roediger, and Mark A. McDaniel. 2014. *Make It Stick: The Science of Successful Learning.* Cambridge: Belknap Press.

Carey, Benedict. 2014. *How We Learn: The Surprising Truth about When, Where, and Why It Happens.* New York: Macmillan.

Carter, Judy. 2013. *The Message of You: Turn Your Life Story into a Money-Making Speaking Career.* New York: St. Martin's Press.

Chiles, Marshall. 2016. *Your Presentation Is a Joke: Using Humor to Maximize Your Impact.* California, CA: CreateSpace Independent Publishing Platform.

Crenshaw, Dave. 2008. *The Myth of Multitasking: How "Doing It All" Gets Nothing Done* San Francisco: Jossey-Bass.

Donovan, Jeremey. 2012. *How to Deliver a TED Talk: Secrets of the World's Most Inspiring Presentations.* California, CA: CreateSpace Independent Publishing Platform.

Duarte, Nancy. 2010. *Resonate: Present Visual Stories That Transform Audiences.* Hoboken: John Wiley & Sons.

Foer, Joshua. 2012. *Moonwalking with Einstein: The Art and Science of Remembering Everything.* New York: Penguin Books.

Gallo, Carmine. 2017. *Talk Like TED: The 9 Public Speaking Secrets of the World's Top Minds*. Australia, NSW: Generic Publications.

Gitomer, Jeffrey H. 2009. *Jeffrey Gitomer's Little Green Book of Getting Your Way: How to Speak, Write, Present, Persuade, Influence, and Sell Your Point of View to Others*. Upper Saddle River, NJ: FT Press.

Gladwell, Malcolm. 2011. *Outliers: The Story of Success*. New York: Back Bay Books.

Hall, Kindra. 2019. *Stories That Stick: How Storytelling Can Captivate Customers, Influence Audiences, and Transform Your Business*. New York: HarperCollins Leadership.

Heath, Chip, and Dan Heath. 2008. *Made to Stick: Why Some Ideas Take Hold and Others Come Unstuck*. London: Random House Publishing Group.

Hogshead, Sally. 2010. *Fascinate: Your 7 Triggers to Persuasion and Captivation*. New York: Harper Business.

Ivey, Andrew. 2010. *Perfect Presentations: How You Can Master the Art of Successful Presenting*. Aldie, VA: Henry.

Keyes, John-Michael. 2011. *Carpe Audience: Give Better Presentations Despite PowerPoint*. California, CA: CreateSpace Independent Publishing Platform.

Lang, James M. 2021. *Small Teaching: Everyday Lessons from the Science of Learning*. 2nd edition. San Francisco: Jossey-Bass.

Luna, Tania, and LeeAnn Renninger. 2015. *Surprise: Embrace the Unpredictable and Engineer the Unexpected*. New York: TarcherPerigee.

Medina, John. 2008. *Brain Rules: 12 Principles for Surviving and Thriving at Work, Home, and School*. Fall River, MA: Pear Press, Reprint edition.

Miller, Fred E. 2011. *No Sweat Public Speaking! How to Develop, Practice, and Deliver a Knock Your Socks off Presentation with No Sweat.* Self-published.

Nater, Swen, and Ronald Gallimore. 2005. *You Haven't Taught until They Have Learned: John Wooden's Teaching Principles and Practices.* Morgantown, WV: Fitness Info Tech.

Neil Sr., Richard H. 2011. *Police Instructor: Deliver Dynamic Presentations, Create Engaging Slides, & Increase Active Learning.* California, CA: CreateSpace Independent Publishing.

Nihill, David. 2016. *Do You Talk Funny?: 7 Comedy Habits to Become a Better (and Funnier) Public Speaker.* Dallas: BenBella Books.

Parr, Ben. 2015. *Captivology: The Science of Capturing People's Attention.* San Francisco: HarperOne.

Pease, Allan, and Barbara Pease. 2006. *The Definitive Book of Body Language.* New York: Bantam Books.

Pollack, John. 2015. *Shortcut: How Analogies Reveal Connections, Spark Innovation, and Sell Our Greatest Ideas.* New York: Avery Reprint edition.

Reynolds, Garr. 2011. *Presentation Zen: Simple Ideas on Presentation Design and Delivery.* 2nd edition. Indianapolis: New Riders.

Reynolds, Garr. 2013. *Presentation Zen Design: A Simple Visual Approach to Presenting in Today's World.* 2nd edition. Indianapolis: New Riders.

Walker, TJ. 2009. *TJ Walker's Secret to Foolproof Presentations.* Austin: Greenleaf Book Group LLC.

Articles and Videos

Baer, Drake. "Blind People Gesture Like Sighted People." The Cut. September 8, 2016. thecut.com/2016/09/blind-people-gesture-like-sighted-people.html.

Baer, Drake. "The Reason Comic Sans Is a Public Good." The Cut. updated August 12, 2020. https://www.thecut.com/2020/08/the-reason-comic-sans-is-a-public-good.html.

Beaumont-Thomas, Ben. "How We Made the Typeface Comic Sans." *The Guardian*, March 28, 2017. https://www.theguardian.com/artanddesign/2017/mar/28/how-we-made-font-comic-sans-typography.

Berk, Ronald A. "Research on PowerPoint: From Basic Features to Multimedia." *International Journal of Technology in Teaching and Learning* 7, no. 1 (2011): 24–35. https://www.ronberk.com/articles/2011_research.pdf.

Berk, Ronald A. "How to Create 'Thriller' PowerPoints in the Classroom!" *Innovative Higher Education* 37, no. 2 (April 2012). DOI: 10.1007/s10755-011-9192-xOnline First.

Blanchard, Ken. "Feedback Is the Breakfast of Champions." Ken Blanchard. August 17, 2009. https://www.kenblanchardbooks.com/feedback-is-the-breakfast-of-champions/.

Bradbury, Neil A. "Attention Span during Lectures: 8 Seconds, 10 Minutes, or More?" *Advances in Physiological Education* 40, no. 4 (October 19, 2016): 509–13. https://journals.physiology.org/doi/pdf/10.1152/advan.00109.2016?dom=prime&src=syn&.

Cision. "Are Declining Attention Spans Killing Your Content Marketing Strategy?" January 22, 2018. https://www.cision.com/us/2018/01/declining-attention-killing-content-marketing-strategy/.

Czekala, Bartosz. "Interleaved Practice—When and How to Use It to Maximize Your Learning Pace." University of Memory. https://universeofmemory.com/interleaved-practice-maximize-learning-pace/.

Covit, Dana. "Comic Sans: The Innocence and Hijacking of a Much-Hated Type." LingoApp. June 5, 2017. https://blog.lingoapp.com/comic-sans-the-innocence-and-hijacking-of-a-much-hated-type-1282b9f74d7f.

Davis, Alison. "19 Quotes That Will Inspire You to Create an Amazing Presentation." Inc. January 21, 2016. https://www.inc.com/alison-davis/19-quotes-that-will-inspire-you-to-create-an-amazing-presentation.html.

Digital Synopsis. "Color Palettes from Famous Movies Show How Colors Set the Mood of a Film." https://digitalsynopsis.com/design/cinema-palettes-famous-movie-colors/.

DeGeneres, Ellen. "Baby Boomers vs. Millennials." The Ellen Show. May 5, 2016. YouTube video, https://www.youtube.com/watch?v=JADG4hXaqy4.

Fell, James S. "The Organic Cereal That Will Change Your Mornings." Chatelaine. Updated November 29, 2013. https://www.chatelaine.com/health/diet/holy-crap-cereal/.

Freeman, Camille. "Are the Images in Your Presentation under Copyright?" Bloom & Grow. August 2014. https://www.camillefreeman.com/2014/08/images-copyright-presentation/.

Goodwin, Bryan. "Research Matters / The Magic of Writing Stuff Down." ASCD. April 1, 2018. http://www.ascd.org/publications/educational-leadership/apr18/vol75/num07/The-Magic-of-Writing-Stuff-Down.aspx.

Greenbaum, Harrison. "Dead Dog in NYC – Stand-Up Comedy." YouTube video, April 4, 2019, https://www.youtube.com/watch?v=8rg4leXrW_o.

Heath, Chip, and Dan Heath. "The Curse of Knowledge." *Harvard Business Review*, December 2006. https://hbr.org/2006/12/the-curse-of-knowledge.

Higbee, Kenneth L. "Recent Research on Visual Mnemonics: Historical Roots and Educational Fruits." *Review of Educational Research* 49, no. 4 (1979): 611–29. https://www.jstor.org/stable/1169987.

Horstman, Mark. "Answering Questions in a Presentation." February 18, 2007. In *Manager-Tools*. Podcast. Podcast audio. https://www.manager-tools.com/2007/02/answering-questions-in-a-presentation-part-1-of-2.

Huizer, Eric Jan. "How to Build Massive Credibility in Your Sales Pitch." Better Marketing. January 18, 2020. https://medium.com/better-marketing/how-do-you-incorporate-credibility-in-your-sales-pitch-847e6bd844d1.

Iconic Fox. "Color in Branding [Infographic]." https://iconicfox.com.au/colour-in-branding-infographic/.

Schumer, Amy. "Amy Schumer – My High School Crush." Just For Laughs. YouTube video, January 23, 2015. https://www.youtube.com/watch?v=YEXmu89_E8o.

LaCroix, Darren. "Ep. 85 Body Language Expert, Blanca Cobb." YouTube video, May 31, 2021. https://www.youtube.com/watch?v=MjVJ-_eOa8M.

LaCroix, Darren. "Ep 208: How to be Funnier with Darren LaCroix." Brand Builders, accessed September 17, 2021. https://brandbuildersgroup.com/tag/darren-lacroix/.

Manager Tools podcast. "The Foundations of Presenting Mastery – Part 1." May 8, 2019. In *Manager Tools*. Podcast. Podcast audio. https://www.manager-tools.com/2016/05/foundations-presenting-mastery-part-1.

Medina, John. "Brain Rule Rundown." Brain Rules. Accessed September 20, 2021. http://brainrules.net/vision/.

Melymbrose, Julia. "20 Creative Presentation Ideas That'll Inspire Audiences to Action in 2021 (+Video)." Envato tuts+. December 30, 2020. https://business.tutsplus.com/tutorials/creative-presentation-ideas--cms-27281.

Mohler, Stanley R. "Quick Response by Pilots Remains Key to Surviving Cabin Decompression." *Flight Safety Foundation Human Factors & Aviation Medicine* 47, no. 1, (Jan–Feb 2000). https://flightsafety.org/hf/hf_jan-feb00.pdf.

Nihill, David. "Presidential Funny That You Can Replicate." David Nihill. May 5, 2016. https://davidnihill.com/presidential-funny-that-you-can-replicate/.

Persaud, Christine. "Bloom's Taxonomy: The Ultimate Guide." Top Hat. February 25, 2021. https://tophat.com/blog/blooms-taxonomy-ultimate-guide/.

Pilon, Annie. "Holy Crap: A Cereal That's out of This World. Literally." Small Biz Trends. May 10, 2014. https://smallbiztrends.com/2014/05/holy-crap-cereal.html.

Police Activity Archive. "The Calmest Cop Ever Gives the Angriest Motorist a Ticket—1992." YouTube video, March 21, 2018. https://www.youtube.com/watch?v=HnWy3Eh352w.

Pogue, David. "Aspect Ratio: A Brief History of Aspect Ratios, aka Screen Proportions." *Scientific American*, February 20, 2018. https://www.scientificamerican.com/article/a-brief-history-of-aspect-ratios-aka-screen-proportions/.

Prisco, Jacopo. "The Game-Changing Typeface Made to Go Unnoticed." CNN. updated March 30, 2020. https://www.cnn.com/style/article/helvetica-60-years/index.html.

Roque, Celine (CX). "How to Make a Persuasive PowerPoint Presentation (With Powerful Tips)." Envato tuts+. May 23, 2019. https://business .tutsplus.com/tutorials/how-to-make-a-persuasive-powerpoint-presentation--cms-25459.

"David Lee Roth tells the story behind the 'no brown M&Ms' legend." YouTube video, February 14, 2012, https://www.youtube.com/ watch?v=_IxqdAgNJck.

Sims, Rowan. "Composition Tips for Drawing the Viewer's Eye through Your Photographs." Digital Photography School. Accessed September 16, 2021. https://digital-photography-school.com/ composition-tips-drawing-viewers-eye-through-your-photographs/.

Spitz, Mark. "The Inquisition: Tough Questions for Martin Gore," *SPIN* magazine, March 26, 2009. https://www.spin.com/2009/03/ inquisition-tough-questions-martin-gore/.

Stambor, Zak. "How Laughing Leads to Learning." *Monitor on Psychology* 27, no. 7 (June 2006). https://www.apa.org/monitor/ jun06/learning.

Cuddy, Amy. "Your Body Language May Shape Who You Are." TED, June 2012, https://www.ted.com/talks/amy_cuddy_your_body_language_ may_shape_who_you_are?language=en/.

Pollack, John. "The Hidden Power of Analogy." Tedx Talks. Tedx U of M. YouTube video, March 9, 2018. https://www.youtube.com/ watch?v=CvnmU2JGUHg.

Robinson, Mark. "How to Present to Keep Your Audience's Attention." TEDx Talks. TEDx Eindhoven. YouTube video, August 4, 2016. https:// www.youtube.com/watch?v=BmEiZadVNWY&t=2s.

Thiagarajan, Sivasailam. "Rapid Training Design 8. Align the Four Training Components." LinkedIn. August 27, 2019. https://www.linkedin.com/pulse/rapid-training-design-8-align-four-components-sivasailam-thiagarajan/.

Valentine, Craig. "5 Ways to Ignite Your Audience with Your Introduction." Craig Valentine MBA. January 22, 2016. https://craigvalentine.com/5-ways-to-ignite-your-audience-with-your-introduction-2/.

Noel, Wanda, and Jordan Snel. "Copyright Matters." Council of Ministers of Education, Canada. 2016. https://www.cmec.ca/139/Copyright.html.

Westbury, Chris and Geoff Hollis. "Wriggly, Squiffy, Lummox, and Boobs: What Makes Some Words Funny?" *Journal of Experimental Psychology* 148, no. 1 (January 2019): 97–123. https://pubmed.ncbi.nlm.nih.gov/30335445/.

William, David K. "Science Proves Funny People Are More Intelligent." Lifehack. https://www.lifehack.org/344730/science-proves-funny-people-are-more-intelligent.

Wolff, Mark. "Cabin Decompression and Hypoxia." TheAirlinePilots.com. https://www.theairlinepilots.com/forumarchive/aeromedical/decompressionandhypoxia.php.

ENDNOTES

1   John Medina, "Brain Rule Rundown," Brain Rules, accessed September 20, 2021, http://brainrules.net/vision/.

2   Nancy Duarte, *Resonate: Present Visual Stories that Transform Audiences* (Hoboken: John Wiley & Sons, 2010).

3   Microsoft Canada, "Attention Spans," Spring 2015, https://dl.motamem.org/microsoft-attention-spans-research-report.pdf.

4   Ibid.

5   Neil A. Bradbury, "Attention Span during Lectures: 8 Seconds, 10 Minutes, or More?," *Advances in Psychology Education* 40, no. 4 (October 19, 2016): 509–13. https://journals.physiology.org/doi/pdf/10.1152/advan.00109.2016?dom=prime&src=syn&.

6   John Medina, *Brain Rules: 12 Principles for Surviving and Thriving at Work, Home, and School* (Fall River, MA: Pear Press, 2008).

7   Michael Auzenne and Mark Horstman, "The Foundations of Presenting Mastery – Part 1," in Manager Tools podcast, produced by Career Tools, podcast audio, May 8, 2019, https://www.manager-tools.com/2016/05/foundations-presenting-mastery-part-1.

8   Will Petty, "Ep21," *Be Effective Podcast*, Podcast Audio, January 26, 2021, http://itunes.appple.com.

9   Malcolm Gladwell, *Outliers: The Story of Success* (New York: Back Bay Books, 2011).

10 Mark Spitz, "The Inquisition: Tough Questions for Martin Gore," *SPIN* magazine, March 26, 2009, https://www.spin.com/2009/03/inquisition-tough-questions-martin-gore/.

11 Fred E. Miller, *No Sweat Public Speaking! How to Develop, Practice, and Deliver a Knock Your Socks off Presentation with No Sweat* (Self-pub., 2011).

12 Sivasailam Thiagarajan, "Rapid Training Design 8. Align the Four Training Components," LinkedIn, August 27, 2019, https://

www.linkedin.com/pulse/rapid-training-design-8-align-four
-components-sivasailam-thiagarajan/.

13 Alison Davis, "19 Quotes That Will Inspire You to Create an
Amazing Presentation," Inc., January 21, 2016, https://www.inc.
com/alison-davis/19-quotes-that-will-inspire-you-to-create-an-
amazing-presentation.html.

14 Patricia Armstrong, "Bloom's Taxonomy," Vanderbilt University
Center for Teaching, https://cft.vanderbilt.edu/guides-sub-pages/
blooms-taxonomy/.

15 Michael Auzenne and Mark Horstman, "The Tyranny of
Unpublished Processes – Part 1," in Manager Tools podcast,
produced by Career Tools, podcast audio, October 21, 2018,
https://www.manager-tools.com/2018/10/tyranny-unpublished
-processes-part-1.

16 "David Lee Roth Tells the Story behind the 'No Brown M&Ms'
Legend," YouTube video. February 14, 2012, https://www.you-
tube.com/watch?v=_IxqdAgNJck.

17 Henry David Thoreau, *The Writings of Henry David Thoreau:
Journal I: 1837–1846*, ed. Bradford Torrey (Cambridge: The
Riverside Press, 1906).

18 Simon Sinek, (@simonsinek), Twitter, May 17, 2020, https://
twitter.com/simonsinek/status/1262010482262769664?lang=en.

19 Robert Baden-Powell, *Scouting for Boys* (Mineola, NY: Dover,
1908), 48.

20 Dave Crenshaw, *The Myth of Multitasking: How "Doing It All" Gets
Nothing Done* (San Francisco: Jossey-Bass, 2008).

21 Rowan Sims, "Composition Tips for Drawing the Viewer's Eye
through Your Photographs," Digital Photography School, accessed September 16, 2021, https://digital-photography-school.
com/composition-tips-drawing-viewers-eye-through-your-photo-
graphs/.

22 *Oxford English Dictionary*, s.v., "serif," accessed September 16,
2021, https://www.lexico.com/en/definition/serif.

23 Jacopo Prisco, "The Game-Changing Typeface Made to Go Unnoticed," CNN, updated March 30, 2020, https://www.cnn.com/style/article/helvetica-60-years/index.html.

24 Ben Beaumont-Thomas, "How We Made the Typeface Comic Sans," *The Guardian*, March 28, 2017, https://www.theguardian.com/artanddesign/2017/mar/28/how-we-made-font-comic-sans-typography.

25 Drake Baer, "The Reason Comic Sans Is a Public Good," The Cut, updated August 12, 2020, https://www.thecut.com/2020/08/the-reason-comic-sans-is-a-public-good.html.

26 Canadian Dyslexia Association, "Voices of Dyslexia: Tragedies & Triumphs," Accessed September 17, 2021, http://www.dyslexiaassociation.ca/english/files/voices.pdf.

27 Andrew Ivey, *Perfect Presentations: How You Can Master the Art of Successful Presenting* (Aldie, VA: Henry, 2010).

28 Matthew Wilson, "12 Bob Ross Quotes That Will Brighten Your Day." Insider, April 1, 2020, https://www.insider.com/bob-ross-quotes-to-brighten-your-day-2020-4.

29 Douglas Jehl, "C.I.A. Nominee Wary of Budget Cuts," *New York Times*, February 3, 1993, https://www.nytimes.com/1993/02/03/us/cia-nominee-wary-of-budget-cuts.html.

30 John Pollack, "The Hidden Power of Analogy," Tedx Talks, Tedx U of M, YouTube video, March 9, 2018, https://www.youtube.com/watch?v=CvnmU2JGUHg.

31 *The Simpsons*, S4:E8, "New Kid on the Block," Wesley Archer, Matt Groening, et al, November 12, 1992, Fox Studios.

32 Police Activity Archive, "The Calmest Cop Ever Gives the Angriest Motorist a Ticket—1992," YouTube video, March 21, 2018, https://www.youtube.com/watch?v=HnWy3Eh352w.

33 Annie Pilon, "Holy Crap: A Cereal That's out of This World. Literally," Small Biz Trends, May 10, 2014, https://smallbiztrends.com/2014/05/holy-crap-cereal.html.

34   Kindra Hall, *Stories That Stick: How Storytelling Can Captivate Customers, Influence Audiences, and Transform Your Business* (New York: Harper Collins, 2019).

35   Ibid.

36   Quentin Tarantino, dir., *Pulp Fiction*, (1994; Miramax Films), 154 min.

37   Stanley R. Mohler, "Quick Response by Pilots Remains Key to Surviving Cabin Decompression," *Flight Safety Foundation Human Factors & Aviation Medicine* 47, no. 1 (Jan–Feb 2000), https://flightsafety.org/hf/hf_jan-feb00.pdf.

38   Chip Heath and Dan Heath, "The Curse of Knowledge," *Harvard Business Review*, December 2006, https://hbr.org/2006/12/the-curse-of-knowledge.

39   Erika Tucker, "Calgary Air Pollution over Last Day Equal to 4hrs in Car with Smoker: Online Tool," Global News, updated August 26, 2015, https://globalnews.ca/news/2187426/calgary-air-pollution-over-last-day-equal-to-smoking-over-50-cigarettes-online-tool/.

40   Richard Branson, *Business Stripped Bare: Adventures of a Global Entrepreneur* (New York: Portfolio, 2011).

41   Kenneth L. Higbee, "Recent Research on Visual Mnemonics: Historical Roots and Educational Fruits," *Review of Educational Research* 49, no. 4 (1979): 611–29, https://www.jstor.org/stable/1169987.

42   Wikipedia. 2021. "Starbucks." Last modified December 3, 2021. https://en.wikipedia.org/wiki/Starbucks#:~:text=Starbucks%20Corporation%20is%20an%20American%20coffee%20company%20and,2019%2C%20the%20company%20operates%20over%2030%2C000%20locations%20worldwide.

43   "Starbucks Tenant Overview."Net Lease Advisor. August 11, 2021. https://www.netleaseadvisor.com/tenant/starbucks-coffee/#:~:text=The%20average%20Starbucks%20store%20size%20varies%20depending%20on,is%20adaptable%20to%20a%20variety%20of%20alternative%20uses.

44 Trolly Wright. "These maps show just how big Central Park is." TimeOut. August 7. 2015. https://www.timeout.com/newyork /blog/these-maps-show-just-how-big-central-park-really- is-080715.

45 Peter C. Brown, Henry L. Roedinger, and Mark A. Daniel, *Make It Stick: The Science of Successful Living* (Cambridge: Belknap Press, 2014).

46 Joseph Joubert. *Joubert: A Selection from His Thoughts.* New York: Dodd, Mead & Co., 1899

47 Brown, Roedinger, and Daniel, *Make It Stick.*

48 Brown, Roedinger, and Daniel, *Make It Stick.*

49 Zak Stambor, "How Laughing Leads to Learning." *Monitor on Psychology* 27, no. 7 (June 2006), https://www.apa.org/monitor/ jun06/learning.

50 Judy Carter. *The Message of You: Turn Your Life Story into a Money-Making Speaking Career.* New York: St. Martin's Press, 2013.

51 *Johnny Carson on Comedy*, "Likability," (Laugh.com, 2006), 64 min.

52 Chris Westbury and Geoff Hollis, "Wriggly, Squiffy, Lummox, and Boobs: What Makes Some Words Funny?," *Journal of Experimental Psychology* 148, no. 1 (January 2019): 97–123, https://pubmed. ncbi.nlm.nih.gov/30335445/.

53 Harrison Greenbaum, "Dead Dog in NYC – Stand-Up Comedy," YouTube video, April 4, 2019, https://www.youtube.com/ watch?v=8rg4leXrW_o.

54 David Nihil, "Presidential Funny That You Can Replicate," David Nihill, May 5, 2016, https://davidnihill.com/ presidential-funny-that-you-can-replicate/.

55 Angie Drobnic Holan, "Obama Says the One Department Regulates Salmon in Freshwater …" Politifact, January 26, 2011, https:// www.politifact.com/factchecks/2011/jan/26/barack-obama/ obama-says-one-department-regulates-salmon-freshwa/.

56 David Nihil, *Do You Talk Funny?: 7 Comedy Habits to Become a Better (and Funnier) Public Speaker* (Dallas: BenBella Books, 2016).

57 Darren LaCroix, "Ep 208: How to be Funnier with Darren LaCroix," accessed September 17, 2021, in Brand Builders podcast, podcast audio, https://brandbuildersgroup.com/tag/darren-lacroix/.

58 Bob Golen (@BobGolen), Tweet, May 8, 2021, https://twitter.com/bobgolen/status/1391204759005286402?lang=fa.

59 Jeffrey H. Gitomer, *Jeffrey Gitomer's Little Green Book of Getting Your Way: How to Speak, Write, Present, Persuade, Influence, and Sell Your Point of View to Others* (Upper Saddle River, NJ: FT Press, 2009).

60 Amy Schumer, "Amy Schumer – My High School Crush," Just for Laughs, YouTube video, January 23, 2015, https://www.youtube.com/watch?v=YEXmu89_E8o.

61 Will Ferrell (@Will_Ferrell), Twitter, November 4, 2013, https://twitter.com/will___ferrell/status/397546389267152897?lang=en.

62 George Carlin, *Brain Droppings* (New York: Hachette Books, 2015).

63 David Frankel, dir., *The Devil Wears Prada*, (2006; 20th Century Fox), 109 min.

64 Ellen DeGeneres, "Baby Boomers vs. Millennials," The Ellen Show, YouTube video, May 5, 2016, https://www.youtube.com/watch?v=JADG4hXaqy4.

65 Desiderius Erasmus, *Adagia* (1500).

66 Marshall Chiles, *Your Presentation Is a Joke: Using Humor to Maximize Your Impact* (CreateSpace Independent Publishing, 2016).

67 Amy Cuddy, "Your Body Language May Shape Who You Are," TED, June 2012, https://www.ted.com/talks/amy_cuddy_your_body_language_may_shape_who_you_are?language=en/.

68 John Medina, *Brain Rules*.

69 Serguei Shcheglov, "Did You Know That There Are More Trees On Earth Than Stars In The Milky Way?" World Atlas, March 13, 2019. https://www.worldatlas.com/articles/did-you-know-that-there-are-more-trees-on-earth-than-stars-in-the-milky-way.html.

70 Kurian M. Tharakan, "Want Someone to Like You? Get Them to Do You a Favour!" StrategyPeak, accessed on December 6, 2021. https://strategypeak.com/want-someone-like-get-favour/.

71 Allen Saunders, "Quotable Quotes," *Reader's Digest* (1957).

72 Jay Roach, dir., *Austin Powers: International Man of Mystery*, (1997; New Line Cinema), 91 min.

73 Michelle Obama, *Becoming*. (New York: Crown, 2018).

74 Darren LaCroix, "Ep. 85 Body Language Expert, Blanca Cobb," YouTube video, May 31, 2021, https://www.youtube.com/watch?v=MjVJ-_eOa8M.

75 Allan Pease, and Barbara Pease, *The Definitive Book of Body Language*. New York: Bantam Books, 2006.

76 Brené Brown, *Daring Greatly: How the Courage to Be Vulnerable Transforms the Way We Live, Love, Parent, and Lead* (New York: Avery, 2015).

77 Ralphie May, *Stand Up Master Class,* Performed by Ralphie May. 2010; Los Angeles; The Comedy Store; April 6, 2020. YouTube, https://www.youtube.com/watch?v=7uBB8HncsrU.

78 Mark Robinson, "How to Present to Keep Your Audience's Attention," TEDx Talks, TEDx Eindhoven, YouTube video, August 4, 2016, https://www.youtube.com/watch?v=BmEiZadVNWY&t=2s.

79 Mark Horstman, "Answering Questions in a Presentation," February 18, 2007, in Manager-Tools Podcast, produced by Career Tools, podcast audio, https://www.manager-tools.com/2007/02/answering-questions-in-a-presentation-part-1-of-2.

80 Mark Brown, and Darren LaCroix. "Five Closing Mistakes". Unforgettable Presentations. March 4, 2021. Podcast. 31:00. Unforgettable Presentations: Five Closing Mistakes on Apple Podcasts

81 Joshua Foer, *Moonwalking with Einstein: The Art and Science of Remembering Everything* (New York: Penguin Books, 2012).

82 "2020 Mass Shooting Statistics," Mass-Shootings.info, November 26, 2021, http://mass-shootings.info/statistics.php?year=2020.

83 Michael Crichton, *Timeline* (New York: Ballantine Books, 2016).

84 Ronald A. Berk, "How to Create 'Thriller' PowerPoints® in the Classroom!," *Innovative Higher Education* 37, no. 2, (April 2012) DOI: 10.1007/s10755-011-9192-xOnline First.

85 Chris Brewer, *Music and Learning: Seven Ways to Use Music in the Classroom*. Tequesta, Florida: LifeSounds, 1995.

86 Swen Nater and Ronald Gallimore, *You Haven't Taught until They Have Learned: John Wooden's Teaching Principles and Practices* (Morgantown, WV: Fitness Info Tech, 2005).

87 Mark Brown, and Darren LaCroix. "The Legendary Brian Tracy". Unforgettable Presentations. July 22, 2021. Podcast. 45:00. Unforgettable Presentations: The Legendary Brian Tracy on Apple Podcasts.

88 Ken Blanchard, "Feedback Is the Breakfast of Champions," Ken Blanchard, August 17, 2009, https://www.kenblanchardbooks.com/feedback-is-the-breakfast-of-champions/.